The Worst Rock-and-Roll Records of All Time
A Fan's Guide to the Stuff You Love to Hate

The Worst Rock-and-Roll Records of All Time

A Fan's Guide to the Stuff You Love to Hate

By Jimmy Guterman and Owen O'Donnell

A Citadel Press Book
Published by Carol Publishing Group

A Citadel Press Book
Published by Carol Publishing Group
Citadel Press
is a registered trademark of
Carol Communications, Inc.

Editorial Offices
600 Madison Avenue
New York, NY 10022

Sales & Distribution Offices
120 Enterprise Avenue
Secaucus, NJ 07094

In Canada; Musson Book Company
A division of General Publishing Co. Limited
Don Mills, Ontario

Design by Victore Design Works

Manufactured in the United States of America
10   9   8   7   6   5   4   3   2   1

Carol Publishing Group books are available at special discounts
for bulk purchases, for sales promotions, fund raising, or
educational purposes. Special editions can also be created to
specifications. For details contact: Special Sales Department,
Carol Publishing Group, 120 Enterprise Ave., Secaucus, NJ 07094

Library of Congress Cataloging-in-Publication Data

Guterman, Jimmy.
    The worst rock and roll records of all time : a fan's guide to the
stuff you love to hate / by Jimmy Guterman and Owen O'Donnell.
        p.   cm.
    "A Citadel Press book."
    ISBN 0-8065-1231-8 : $14.95
    1. Rock music—Miscellanea.   2. Rock music—Discography.   3. Rock
music—Humor.   I. O'Donnell, Owen.   II. Title.
ML3534.G88   1991
781.66'026'6—dc20   91-15468
                                                          CIP
                                                          MN

For Jane Kokernak
and David and Arthur

If you can't annoy somebody, there's little point in writing.
—**Kingsley Amis**

CONTENTS

ACKNOWLEDGMENTS

For their encouragement and support, we thank James Austin, Paul Kingsbury and Ronnie Pugh at the Country Music Foundation, Elizabeth Geiser, Kathleen M. Hansen, Hank and Monica Hubbard, Linda Hubbard, Bob Hyde, Carmel Landino, Noel and Janice Monk, Matthew O'Connell, Tim Riley, Lydia Sherwood, Gary Stewart, and Dave Weiner.

Thanks to Mark Caro for reading an early manuscript and offering comments that were consistently incisive and funny. We promise him that the Chartreuse Microbus version of "Rainbow Rhinoceros" will make it into the next volume.

Thanks to Reed Lappin for the Elvis tape and everyone at In Your Ear! in Boston for general support.

No thanks to Charlie "Artless" Conrad for starting this whole thing.

On the publishing side, we are grateful to Steven Schragis, Bruce Bender, Dan Levy, Steven Brower, and everyone else at Carol, whose enthusiasm has been contagious.

Personal thanks to John Guterman, the Scheys, the O'Donnells, the extended Bender clan, and the Kokernaks.

All chart positions come from Joel Whitburn's Record Research library of *Billboard* chart information. All factual errors are ours.

We're writing this book not because we want to, but because we have to. You see, we love this stuff. We've come to praise, not to bury. Better yet, we've come to exhume—and switch the bodies in the graves.

An important part of being a good rock-and-roll fan is reveling in songs so laughable it's hard to believe any sane record company released them. When you listen to a track like "All I Have to Do Is Dream," the Everly Brothers classic as desecrated in a tuneless lovebird duet by Andy Gibb and Victoria Principal, the only reason your jaw isn't on the ground with shock is that you're laughing so hard. For those who love the music, what's stuck at the bottom of the barrel offers otherworldly pleasures. This book is for rock-and-roll fans who haven't let their tastes or their attitudes get too stuffy.

We have two goals here: to be funny and to infuriate. Rock and roll is unlike most other pop-culture forms (especially film) in that there is no consensus as to who the lowliest practitioners are. Thanks to the Medved brothers, every smartass high-school kid with an interest in cinema knows about *Plan 9 from Outer Space*, the career of Sonny Tufts, and mysterious alternate endings to *The Exorcist, II*. Rock and roll isn't like that, nor should it be. There's some agreement among rock critics concerning rock and roll's greatest albums (Bob Dylan's *Blonde on Blonde*, the Beatles' *Rubber Soul*, Chuck Berry's *Golden Decade*, and Elvis's *Sun Sessions* usually figure prominently on the most thoughtful lists, and we'd stick in Rod Stewart's *Every Picture Tells a Story*), but after that, opinions diverge wildly, even between the two of us.

In 1987, when *Rolling Stone* conducted a survey among its critics that resulted in its "100 Best Albums of the Last 20 Years" issue (a poll to which one of us contributed), album twenty-five was the debut record by the Doors, who also happen to one of our least favorite allegedly definitive units. During the Doors revival that has been going on nonstop since Jim Morrison croaked in 1971, we Doors-haters have remained convinced that Jimbo was a stillborn doggereler and an overwrought singer and that his cohorts sounded like a group on loan from the local Econ-o-Lodge cocktail room. Ray Manzarek's organ reduced the dark drones of the Velvet Underground to a heavy-rock cliché; drummer John Densmore wouldn't recognize a beat if you spotted him the *b*, the *e*, the *t*, and then let him buy a vowel. Guitarist Robbie Krieger was the band's lone semicompetent, though his workouts had to cut back to make room for the sludge surrounding him. And not having a bassist to pace the songs limited Manzarek even more. The overextended noodler was so busy approximating bass lines with his left hand that he could do little more than alternate upper-octave chords with his right. On top of all this desperate thumping, Morrison bellowed hit-and-miss images of anger, lust, angst, ego, boredom, petulance, and more petulance, so unfocused that Rod McKuen would have blushed. Too often the Doors were content to pump up Morrison's Lizard King legend without releasing songs to justify it. They were perfect for a posthumous revival, because none of the high-school kids turned rock critics and FM disc jockeys who put them back on the charts in the eighties could have remembered how dull the band was in the first place.

We've probably already lost some of you. "How dare these creeps make fun of the coolest band of all time!" you're screaming. Well, shut up: now you know what we're after. (Although we ought to acknowledge that Manzarek eventually found a reason to live, producing some magnificent records for the Los Angeles punk band X.) This is a casual book, but it's also a revisionist history of rock and roll, one in which esteemed artists are allowed to be human and make mistakes and one in which overhyped schlocksters get their due. You might put our favorite bands in your garbage can. Many of the performers we banish to "worst" categories regularly sell millions of copies of their every release. Chances are we'll exasperate many of you. That's fine. If you can't argue about rock and roll, what can you argue about?

As rock and roll has aged and become more "serious," it has developed a herd of sacred cows. Nobody dares make fun of rock's elder statesmen. Nobody explodes the pretentions of today's *artistes*.

We, on the other hand, live for that.

While we have no qualms about being nearly malicious when the situation calls for it (as you'll note every time the names Phil Collins and Billy Joel appear), we will also be careful to place our dubious commendations in context. When we label Chuck Berry's "My Ding-a-Ling" one of the worst rock-and-roll singles of all time, we will also celebrate how ground-breaking and influential his earlier work was—which makes the fact that "My Ding-a-Ling" was his only number-one single all the more heartbreaking.

So we offer you fight fodder, bathroom reading material, and dissections of "music" that probably won't be celebrated in next year's Rock-and-Roll Hall of Fame induction ceremonies (at least not if they let us vote). Some of the records in this book are legendarily awful; some of them are thought by many to be among the finest records ever (over)produced. What do you think?

How does a record become one of the worst rock-and-roll records of all time? It's not easy. Just as a true masterpiece often emerges from deep, nearly unconscious ideas (we're thinking of recordings as diverse as Van Morrison's *Astral Weeks* and Claudine Clark's "Party Lights"), so too do the most god-awful works frequently emanate from ill-guided, unspoken ideas at the artist's core. These records are often intensely personal and deeply felt, although sometimes they're so insular that the only people who have a clue as to what the songs are about are the songwriters. As a result, the performer bypasses the internal artistic censor/bullshit detector that usually kicks in long before he or she books studio time. In that sense, their most wrongheaded work can tell us far more about performers than can their top-rank stuff.

The criteria for being considered one of the worst rock-and-roll records of all time are quite strict. The two main elements are control and stature. The artist must have at least passively condoned the project, and the work must be by a "major" artist (any schlub can put out a wretched record), although a notably bad performance will sometimes lower the stature requirement. Left out are compilations with no artist input, except for any Elvis Presley set, which, given the crap that came out under his name when he was alive, we can safely assume the King would have permitted. We'll have no novelty records, unless the novelty aspect is inadvertent or had something to do with "The Beverly Hillbillies." For our purposes, a miserable record by a great performer (say, Bob Dylan) is far more interesting than the latest garbage installment from a hack (say, Neil Diamond).

As you make your way through this volume, you'll also notice a great preponderance of music from the seventies and eighties, with the fifties and sixties getting somewhat short shrift. As the rock-and-roll music industry grew larger in the more recent decades, there was simply more room for junk. There were many terrifyingly bad rock-and-roll recordings mastered in the fifties and sixties, and we will touch on them, but for sheer quantity the seventies and eighties go unchallenged. (As we write, the *Billboard* singles charts are limping through an unusually weak period. Except for paying tribute to Milli Vanilli, whose horridity was timeless even before the true singers' identities were revealed, we will refrain from commenting on current records, whose awfulness has not yet stood the test of time. As veteran bottom-of-the-barrel rock lyricist Sammy Hagar has bellowed, "Only time will tell/If we stand the test of time.")

Finally, a main motive for writing this book is that since we were born in the early sixties, bad records of the seventies in particular have scarred us for life. Permit us, if you will, this book-length exorcism.

If you violate these rules, you will make bad rock and roll and a couple of guys looking for a quick buck will write about you.

1. Do not retain a band's name if the most important member(s) has left the group. Does anybody (even Pete Townshend) really like anything the Who have recorded since Keith Moon died in 1978?

2. Do not sing a song about Elvis, especially if you have never been in a recording studio before.

3. Do not record for Arista Records. In the late eighties, Clive Davis's label was a haven for art-rock has-beens eager for one last pillage, like GTR and the Kantner-Balin-Casady Band (both of which broke up after one album) and Anderson, Bruford, Wakeman, Howe (pending). Arista's flagship "new" artists of the time, particularly Milli Vanilli, were cynical exploitation units.

4. Rock-and-roll songs with an orchestral choir are bound to be horrible. (Sole exception: the Rolling Stones' "You Can't Always Get What You Want.")

5. Rock lyrics are not poetry (especially if Sting or Bono writes them).

6. The quality of a rock-and-roll song is inversely proportional to the number of instruments on it (unless you're Van Morrison).

7. Supergroups never are.

8. Rock stars are not actors.

9. Actors are not rock stars.

10. White rock-and-roll stars who talk about their R&B roots are probably lying. Similarly, anyone born after April 1954 who records at the Sun Studio is a poseur. Furthermore, a return to roots is not necessarily a good thing. Listened to John Lennon's *Rock 'n' Roll* lately?

11. Don't sing a song about your dead parent, especially if that parent was a celebrity. This is the Hank Williams, Jr., rule.

12. Elvis is dead.

13. Do not go to art school.

14. The more controversial the cause embraced, the more likely the star may actually be committed to it. Do you know anyone in favor of hunger or homelessness?

15. Whatever you do, Jerry Lee Lewis has already done it. Probably better, too.

16. A list is not a song. (Most blatant recent violation: Billy Joel's evasive "We Didn't Start the Fire.")

17. Established artists should not allow family members into the band.

18. There is no reason besides greed for an established performer to accept corporate sponsorship.

19. Live records should reflect what a performance actually sounded like when it occurred. We loved the Talking Heads' *Stop Making Sense* until we found out how many studios were used for postproduction.

20. Videos are commercials.

21. Good politics are not what make good lyrics.

22. Formidable technical proficiency is never sufficient. This rule explains why art rock is always bad.

23. Neither is formidable hair. (Exception: Little Richard.)

24. Do not hang out with Jeff Lynne or Dave Stewart. They will produce your record, you will have to take part in periodic psychedelic revivals, and you'll start dressing like them. Do you want to wear a paisley vest and cowboy boots that badly?

25. Cult artists are frequently just as boring and predictable as mainstream ones. This is also called the Robyn Hitchcock rule.

26. Heavy metal should be fast.

27. Punk happened. (Note tense.)

28. If you have recorded more than three albums, someone will some day compile a boxed set dedicated to your oeuvre and *Rolling Stone* will give it four stars and call it a "grand summary, especially valuable on pristine CD."

29. The Rock and Roll Hall of Fame is an oxymoron. If you want your work to be recognized in a museum, learn to paint.

30. Admit you're balding.

31. Love is not all you need. Psychedelic lyrics never ring true after you've come down.

32. Do not record cover versions of Motown or Stax/Volt hits.

33. Rock and roll is but one small part of the music being made on this planet. Rockers who think they're changing the world are in fact only reaching a small part of it.

33⅓. Do not die before Albert Goldman.

The Fifty Worst Rock-and-Roll Singles of All Time

JOHN COUGAR
"Jack and Diane"
Riva, 1982
highest chart position: number one (four weeks)

John Mellencamp is one of the most significant American rock performers of the late eighties. Since his 1983 breakthrough *Uh Huh*, he's supported causes as worthy and diverse as Farm Aid, Chess Studios, Mitch Ryder, and James McMurtry and has been a probing writer, peerless bandleader, and inventive producer.

Before then, of course, he sucked. Everything the former Johnny Cougar wrote or sang rang false or stolen, and his desire to write Big Statements was surpassed only by his inability to pull them off. The most hilarious (and, alarmingly, most commercially successful) of his failed summations of life was "Jack and Diane."

Like Meat Loaf half a decade before, Cougar filled (less snugly) the market gap created by Bruce Springsteen's trademark inability to take less than a lifetime to make a rock record (1982's *Nebraska* is wonderful, but as a solo acoustic record with no hit singles it doesn't count here). The rock audience has a natural desire for "honest" songs about "real life," sung with "emotion" by a "working-class hero" from the "heartland." Cougar was from Indiana, so he qualified for the heartland attribute. Everything else, though, was a sham.

"Jack and Diane" is an extremely little ditty about two teenagers having sex, but leave it to Cougar to try to build that into a grand pronouncement on, you guessed it, America. Cougar tries to wrap it all together with the straining-to-be-meaningful couplet "Life goes on/ Long after the thrill of living is gone." Which means what? That life goes on long after you die? The line is supposed to refer to aging gracefully (a concept repudiated by the far superior "Authority Song"), but it doesn't sound like Cougar believes what he is singing. We mistrust this world-weary cynicism coming from a rock star only in his early thirties; we also question the logic of the garbled statement. Did Cougar really mean to sing "Life goes on/Long after the pill of giving is wan"? It makes just as much sense, as does "Life goes on/Long after the thrill of eating Szechuan."

Ah, that must be it: a song about two kids in the American heartland in the back seat of a '57 Chevy munching kung pao chicken. Go get 'em, Johnny.

IRENE RYAN
"Granny's Mini-Skirt"
NashWood, 1965
highest chart position: did not chart

This bluegrass knockoff isn't Flatt and Scruggs, but it sure is flat.

After years of toiling in Equity obscurity, veteran actress Irene Ryan scored in the early 1960s when she landed the lead role of Granny on "The Beverly Hillbillies" (or maybe we should say that she hit "black gold, Texas tea"). Granny wasn't the first of television's sprightly old ladies and unfortunately she wasn't the last, but that doesn't excuse this feeble attempt to capitalize on her newfound success.

For anyone who claims they don't "get" bluegrass music, we suggest a little exercise. First play any Bill Monroe song; it doesn't matter which one, just put it on. Then listen to Granny's song. You've just had every lesson you'll ever need in understanding the difference between what works in bluegrass and what never will. Uninspired fiddle, banjo, and acoustic guitar picking are dominant, while the Markleys' backing vocals (or as the label says, "Vocal Background") sound like the singers failed the audition to audition for "Hee-Haw." To be fair, Ryan acquits herself fairly well as an actress on this. At no point do we doubt that she is the brain-dead honky-tonk fashion victim portrayed on the picture sleeve in said skirt and fishnet stockings.

Oh yes, the words. Seems that ol' Granny wears a mini-skirt. ("When I do the twist and jerk/It drives ol' Grandpa wild." Sure.) This attire freaks out Grandpa, who says that it's either a new outfit or a new spouse. ("He can't stand to stare at my bony knees.") Granny acquiesces.

"Granny's Mini-Skirt" is the perfect record for someone who likes sexual stereotypes, regional stereotypes, and anorexic bluegrass rhythms. As for us, we're wondering if perhaps the wrong granny got run over by that reindeer.

THE EVERLY BROTHERS
"Ebony Eyes"
Warner Brothers, 1961
highest chart position: number eight

Del Shannon and Gary U.S. Bonds

notwithstanding, rock and roll was in rough shape in 1961. Buddy Holly was dead, Chuck Berry was in jail, Jerry Lee Lewis had been banished, and Elvis was making *Blue Hawaii.* As awful as each of these fates was for the artists involved and for rock and roll as a whole, a fate just as horrifying befell the Everly Brothers during this same period.

They changed record companies.

From 1957 to 1960, while toiling in Nashville for Cadence Records, Don and Phil Everly recorded some of the most vivid songs about teenage life ever put down on vinyl. Whether singing about the joys of young love ("Devoted to You," "('Til) I Kissed You") or the tribulations of dealing with school and parents ("Problems," "Wake Up, Little Susie"), they always brought an honesty to the material that few could duplicate. Play the Everlys' "When Will I Be Loved" back-to-back with Linda Ronstadt's unctuous cover and you'll hear what we mean.

During 1960, the brothers switched to Hollywood's Warner Brothers Records. Their first release for the monolith, "Cathy's Clown," turned out to be the duo's biggest seller ever, moving more than two million copies long before platinum became the industry standard. Almost immediately things began to go downhill, and "Ebony Eyes" represents how far the boys could fall.

"Ebony Eyes" is the Everly Brothers' attempt to present a teen tragedy, a category of pop song then in vogue. The standard characteristics of such songs were (1) the happy couple, (2) the untimely death of one-half of the happy couple (the more gruesome the better), and (3) the projected reunion of the once and future happy couple in the afterlife. "Ebony Eyes" fills the bill in all respects.

Against the background of an angelic choir (a…er…dead giveaway of how the song is going to turn out), the boys sing the sad tale of a soldier waiting at the airport for his fiancée's plane to arrive so they can get married. During the spoken passage in the middle of the song—that is, long after the rest of us have figured out how the story will end—the poor sucker wonders why the plane is late. Then comes the instant of recognition (as the ominous, annoying drum roll gets louder) when an announcement is made asking those waiting for flight 1203 to report to the chapel across the street. The first question that comes to our minds is, across the street from where? The airport? Where is this airport anyway—in the middle of downtown? We're not sure if our hero even bothers going to the chapel. He's so sure she's dead that he's already begun fantasizing about their heavenly reunion.

"Ebony Eyes" was hardly the worst entry in the teen tragedy sweepstakes. Unlike the hero of Dickie Lee's 1964 "Patches," the protagonist doesn't decide to off himself right away so he can join his soulmate ASAP. And at least there isn't a scene in which the body is pulled from the twisted, burning, shattered (you get the idea) wreckage, as in both Mark Dining's "Teen Angel" and Ray Peterson's "Tell Laura I Love Her." But we had a right to expect more from the Everly Brothers than from those losers, and that's why they're included here.

GLENN FREY
"The Heat Is On"
MCA, 1984
highest chart position: number two

BOB SEGER
"The Horizontal Bop"
Capitol, 1980
highest chart position: number forty-two

Can't forget the motor city.

In the late seventies and early eighties, no two performers epitomized the reach of Detroit rock and roll—and the dangers of leaving home—more than Glenn Frey and Bob Seger. As a founding member of the Eagles, the quintessential seventies–Southern California–laid-back–mellow-narcissistic–masquerading-as-country-when-appropriate–soft-rock band, Frey portrayed himself as a California superstud displaying a penchant for sexist lyrics and paper-thin arrangements. By the turn of the decade, Seger, a journeyman rocker with an outstanding voice who suffered for years before his much-deserved mid-seventies breakthrough, had also succumbed to the blandness of Hollywood rock.

Frey responded to the breakup of the Eagles by making music that was, amazingly, even less substantial. The artistic and commercial success of Eagles drummer Don Henley's subsequent records indicates where that band's talent was. Also, it's no accident that Henley started to show flashes of brilliance only when he didn't have Frey's simple ideas and simpler guitar chords dogging him around. While Henley's lyrics took on diverse issues with aplomb and his arrangements became far more muscular than anything the weakling Eagles ever worked out, Frey's music and lyrics grew gradually more trivial. On his first solo album, 1982's descriptively titled *No Fun Aloud*, Frey wrote some songs about sad love (all of which sounded like the minor hit "The One You Love") and some songs about happy love (all of which sounded like the even more minor hit "I Found Somebody"). Pretty soon he was writing songs as imaginative as the title "Sexy Girl," and he was also turning Frankie Ford's New Orleans R&B masterpiece "Sea Cruise" into a lazy excuse for his session musician friends to earn triple scale.

Having exhausted what few ideas he took with him from the Eagles (his second LP, *The Allnighter*, didn't even go gold, his first record ever—Eagles or solo—not to do so), Frey opted for a rejuvenation move of many aging rockers in the eighties: he got a gig singing the main song for a mediocre action comedy, in this case Eddie Murphy's *Beverly Hills Cop*. "The Heat Is On" is supposed to be a rocker, but as a speedy soundtrack tune it's no more convincing than Kenny Loggins's twin towers of movie theme stupidity, "Footloose" and "Danger Zone." A drum machine that's probably being played by that darned Energizer rabbit pushes Frey to sound interested in a song that is about nothing. The only thing we find out in this song is that the "heat" somewhere is "on." What heat? We don't know; Frey doesn't care. And where is it on? For all we know, he might be at his vacation home in Aspen telling his honey that the thermostat has kicked in and they can get into the hot tub soon.

Frey's no dope when it comes to making a living. After "The Heat Is On" became a massive hit—something that never would have happened if people didn't associate it with Eddie Murphy hanging off the side of a runaway truck—he tried to solidify his soundtrack credentials. He wrote two songs that wound up on "Miami Vice" episodes (he appeared in one installment) and he appeared in a bad war movie, but he still couldn't get it together without tie-ins: even Irving Azoff's promotion machine couldn't resuscitate Frey's career. Last we heard of him he was doing commercials for soft drinks and health clubs and waiting for a phone call from Henley. Even he didn't take himself seriously anymore.

Seger has lasted much better. His 1983 album *The Distance* stands as a remarkable distillation of his broad rock sources, and he remains a shouter with few peers. But in 1980 Seger's commercial supremacy (*Against the Wind* went to number one) was outmatched only by his remarkable fall into the kind of laid-back rock purveyed by Frey and his ilk. On *Against the Wind* he made two good bands—his live unit, the Silver Bullet Band, and the usually reliable Muscle Shoals Rhythm Section—sound bored. Which makes sense, considering the material. Seger's eagerness to fit in with his new Southern California snooze-rock pals is especially evident on the mild rockers. "Betty Lou's Gettin' Out Tonight" and "Her Strut" are bewilderingly lame ditties from a writer and singer who can often imagine both sides of a relationship. Worse yet, in both songs he sounds like an aging high-school football jerk who never grew out of thinking of "girls" as either virgins or whores. The Eagles influence is obvious.

Seger's inability to rock out on *Against the Wind* is epitomized by the single "The Horizontal Bop." It's a huffy song about sex, one without any danger: high-school boys could sing it as an act of woman-fearing male bonding, while high-school girls could sing it as a goofy song about "doing it" without any dirty words. It's as provocative as shaving cream. Years before the age of safe sex, it's a safe song about sex.

By his next record Seger remembered he was great, so maybe *Against the Wind* was a mistake that won't be repeated (and Seger records so infrequently nowadays he'd probably never get around to repeating the mistake even if he wanted to). But it does go to show that if you don't choose your friends well, you can get yourself into big trouble.

BRYAN ADAMS
"Summer of '69"
A&M, 1985
highest chart position: number five

Bryan Adams's derivativeness is rivaled only by his opportunism. Before he went platinum in 1983 with the album *Cuts Like a Knife* and single "Straight from the Heart" (did we mention that all his titles and ideas are clichés?), the Canadian singer tried everything—from the blandest pop to the most unfunky disco— to make it big. If there's anything that unites Adams's broad, fumbling attempts for fame, it's their consistent falseness. You never believe a word Adams sings or a note he writes because he's just as likely as not to undercut it with the next song or the next line. Finding him on the radio is like discovering a mosquito buzzing in your ear; you quickly swat him away, but you know sometime soon you're going to have to deal with him again.

The most bogus, most derivative, most opportunistic song Adams has thrown at us is "Summer of '69," from his mannered 1984 album *Reckless*. The nostalgia of the song ("When I look back now...those were the best days of my life") quickly turns to petulance, and the one guitar riff that propels the song (Chuck Berry filtered through Bruce Springsteen filtered through John Cafferty filtered through a beer commercial) gets boring long before you've heard it for the hundredth time (somewhere in the second verse). You've heard it all before, done better. The song is about a singer's first band, how intense the moments with the band were, and how the group broke up when one member quit and another got married. For the record, Adams was ten years old in 1969; it took him a while to admit that the song wasn't autobiographical. (C'mon, Bryan: even Jerry Lee wouldn't marry a ten-year-old, and you're more uptight than he'll ever be.)

"Summer of '69" appeared just after sixties nostalgia crested and everyone from the Doors to the Hollies was enjoying the fruits of rediscovery. The sixties nostalgia that sprung up in the mid-eighties was a fraud by industry leaders who refused to divulge to a new generation that the unmatchable music was inextricable from the horrible events that split this country in two as nothing had since the Civil War. Instead, culturally uneducated kids were made to hear songs like Martha and the Vandellas' "Dancing in the Street" and the Rolling Stones' "Street Fighting Man" as no more than party ditties. It's this imagined sixties—one without Vietnam, one without James Earl Ray, one without Altamont—that "Summer of '69" memorializes. Even if the song isn't autobiographical (fine by us; we couldn't care less about Bryan's childhood), it has to sound like someone's real life. Adams's ideas about the sixties are at least third-hand; he can't make the time real for himself, so forget about his making it real for us through his songs.

ROBERT HAZARD
"Escalator of Life"
RCA (reissue of independent release), 1983
highest chart position: number fifty-eight

HOOTERS
"All You Zombies"
Columbia, 1985
highest chart position: number fifty-eight
(Coincidence or supernatural phenomenon? You be the judge.)

Corporate hype isn't necessarily evil, but when a particularly appalling product gets the treatment, it's time to sharpen the daggers. For instance, on a network television video show one Friday night in 1985, the announcer heralded "a new video by that great new band from Philadelphia, the Hooters." They were neither great nor new. Some context:

In 1981, the two biggest-drawing local bands in Philadelphia were Robert Hazard and the Heroes, and the Hooters. Hazard's dress code was Calvin Klein's version of Joey Ramone and he sounded like David Bowie. Alas, the Bowie he chose to emulate was that of "The Laughing Gnome." Hazard put out a hard-rock version of "Blowin' in the Wind" that could have turned Dylan back into a folk purist. He hit it big on MTV with "Escalator of Life" (sample lyric: "We're shopping in the human mall") and never recorded the only good song he ever wrote, "Girls Just Want to Have Fun." One line not covered by Cyndi Lauper: "All my girls are gonna walk in the sun." In our minds, the unquestionable high point of Hazard's brief career occurred when he told an interviewer, completely seriously, "I want my show to be more than just a concert. I want it to be like *E.T.*" He did not mean "Entertainment Tonight."

The Hooters were Hazard's main competition in the fractured Philadelphia club circuit, and their perceived lack of commercial potential gave them a strong street reputation. An indie single, "Fighting on the Same Side," presented a band with equally impressive pop and reggae chops. They never could cut it live, but they lucked into a gig as backup band for Cyndi Lauper's *She's So Unusual*, which led to their own major label deal. Their playing on Lauper's LP was astonishingly empathic, and keyboardist-singer Rob Hyman's cowriting credit for "Time after Time" underlined his band's importance to that record's success.

Their own LP, *Nervous Night*, was competent corporate product, the kinds of music the band used to rail against in the Philly underground press. The sound reeked of Next Big Thing, from gratuitous power chords to Rick Chertoff's sanitized production. The lyrics, most of them by Hyman and guitarist Eric Bazilian, accomplished the dubious feat of cramming nearly every boy-girl rock-and-roll cliché onto one twelve-inch piece of vinyl. The resolution of every musical and lyrical idea was telegraphed far in advance, the performances had the spontaneity of professional wrestling, and the tentative forays into white reggae were about as convincing as Donny Osmond covering Bunny Wailer. (Yeah, we know: "Don't give him ideas.")

The song that attracted the most attention was the bombastic "All You Zombies," in which the subtle reggae of the verses was surrounded and eventually crushed by heavy-metal guitars. The lyrics dropped biblical names like Rona Barrett emerging from a Talmudic retreat, and with equal understanding of the subject matter. "Zombies" was condescending from the title on down: the band distanced itself not only from "all you sittin' in high places," but also from "all you people in the street." It's one thing to announce that you're better than some abstract businessman or politician; it's another to suggest that you're better than the people you want to buy your record. This was a band with a street rep?

Hazard promptly disappeared after his RCA recordings bombed. The Hooters slogged along, eventually falling so low that the only way they could get any attention was by recording with noted rock-haters Peter, Paul, and Mary (we'll get to them later).

PAT BENATAR
"Sex as a Weapon"
Chrysalis, 1985
highest chart position: number twenty-eight

Don't believe the hype; nobody else did. After more than half a decade of making a fortune by cranking out album-oriented-radio ready-mades that accentuated her submissive voice and his aggressive arrangements, singer Pat Benatar (real name: Patricia Andrzejewski) and her husband, producer-guitarist Neil Geraldo, were hungry for some credibility. Benatar had a career plagued by major inconsistencies of intent: she placed her 1980 hit "Hit Me With Your Best Shot" on the same record as "Hell Is for Children," the latter an attempted Big Statement about child abuse. On the cover of *Crimes of Passion* (the album containing these two songs) she wore a tight dance outfit with her butt stuck out for our amusement. Did she want us to hit her, care for her, or ogle her? All paths led to record stores; as long as fans bought the record, she didn't care what message she was putting across.

So it's not surprising that when Benatar and Geraldo wanted to be legitimized, they still tried to have it both ways. As much as they might claim otherwise, the primary purpose of "Sex as a Weapon" (single and video) was to titillate: it was no accident that the first two words of the chorus—"*Stop using* sex as a weapon"—were left off the title and the record sleeve. This way they could damn the idea and still make money promoting it. There were the occasional frowns on sexual exploitation in the lyrics (by future Kodak jingle writers Tom Kelly and Billy Steinberg), but they were always accompanied by a nod and a wink. Pat and Neil filled many interviewers' cassettes with their ramblings about how they were now purveyors of high art, but nobody believed them (however, award them points for signing up with the Sun City Project) and they haven't had a major hit since. If you're making a sincerity move, you had better be believable.

THE JACKSONS
"State of Shock"
Epic, 1984
highest chart position: number three

MICK JAGGER AND DAVID BOWIE
"Dancing in the Street"
EMI America, 1985
highest chart position: number seven

We think he's trivialized his enormous talent beyond belief, but sometimes, we admit, we feel sorry for Michael Jackson. He has to feed that ridiculous chimp, Liza and Liz probably call him at crazy hours, and Janet's managers cut her a better record deal.

One time we really felt sorry for him was in 1984 when his family guilt-tripped him into undergoing one last album and tour with his brothers before he left them for good. (Just to set the record straight, we felt doubly sorry for the audience that was charged thirty bucks for tickets to see the Jacksons shill for Pepsi and perform a perfunctory glitz exercise.) Michael didn't want to cut an album with his brothers, but everyone at Epic knew no one would buy a Jacksons record without him on it (imagine "Ladies and gentlemen: Tito!"), so for the *Victory* album he tossed them an awkward paranoid ballad ("Be Not Always"), contributed a few verses to a marginal dance tune ("Torture"), and promised a big-name duet.

The big name turned out to be Mick Jagger, another titanic performer who was bumbling through a public career crisis at the time. The number they quickly cooked up in the studio, a two-chord rocker called "State of Shock," is so slight it hardly exists: it seems as if the song takes longer to listen to than it did to record. The arrangement is just guitar and drum machine, but instead of being raw, it sounds like a demo that smelled so bad nobody wanted to come close enough to touch it up. Maybe Jackson thought the combination of a guitar-based rock song and a rock-identified performer like Jagger would add up to another "Beat It"-style genre-buster, but all you hear is two professional entertainers hamming it up in the studio. They call and respond to each other's first-thing-that-comes-to-mind lyrics ("You got me para-lyzed/You got me hypnotized") and sound so amused by their own camaraderie-filled collaboration that they never get around to deliver-ing a real vocal. They preen, they pose, but they never sing.

We mean this literally. By the end of the song (that is, by the time they've repeated the first verse enough times that we're all tired of it), Jagger speaks. It's as if Jackson said, "Mick, we need to fill thirty more seconds. Listen, just talk. It doesn't matter what you say. I just sold thirty million *Thrillers*; my fans'll buy anything. Just talk. Nobody'll care." So they tossed this off as quickly as possible and skedaddled. They knew people would buy anything they did together.

Jagger seems to have an affinity for this sort of inconsequential quickie duet. The next year David Bowie called him up to ask him to help out on a single to benefit Live Aid; Jagger jumped at the opportunity. (Remember, this was before anybody knew anything about their alleged collaboration of a decade before.) The song they decided to disembowel was Martha and the Vandellas' signature song, "Dancing in the Street." (Stones fans noted that "Dancing in the Street" provoked "Street Fighting Man.")

As with "State of Shock," the version of "Dancing in the Street" had to be recorded and filmed quickly (in one day), so Jagger and Bowie used spontaneity as an excuse to sound like lounge singers having a laugh. They add unnecessary lyrics at whim (why is Bowie yelling "South America!"?), decline to sing syllables that would necessitate moving their mouths too wide or too fast, and generally slight a song that once meant much to Jagger at least. Their accompaniment is the kind of usual clean, studio-schlock trot that makes us appreciate better the few times nowadays when the Stones get it right.

We commend Jagger and Bowie for donating their time to a worthy cause, but as with Jagger and Jackson on "State of Shock," we question why these major rock figures bothered to turn on the microphones if they didn't have anything to say.

SIMON AND GARFUNKEL
"The Dangling Conversation"
Columbia, 1966
highest chart position: number twenty-five

Lots of overeducated guys say they're poets to pick up girls, and many of them eventually think they are. Paul Simon is no exception. How many got the feeling while watching *Annie Hall* that Simon wasn't acting?

Throughout their tempestuous career, Simon and Garfunkel were always thought of as the one folk group who could bridge the generation gap: they were pseudohip enough for the younger set and pseudointellectual enough for the older. Many have credited Bob Dylan with starting the singer-songwriter genre, but it was actually Simon who made hypersensitivity an inescapable hallmark of the form. "The Dangling Conversation" is the exemplar of Simon's writing during the heyday of Simon and Garfunkel.

Using his best professorial tone (one he still reserves for folks who don't understand why he was morally right to bust a United Nations cultural boycott), Simon relates the story of lovers who can relate to their choices in literature better than to each other. Using the standard clichés of people who tend to overintellectualize everything (the same people who thought Simon and Garfunkel were so wonderful to begin with), Simon falls into his own trap. He's supposedly asking us to feel pity for these people, which makes sense: virtually all Simon and Garfunkel songs—including such dubious classics as "The Boxer" and "I Am a Rock"—are soft requests for pity.

But the only ones you pity after hearing "The Dangling Conversation" are the inner-city kids deprived of a good education who would certainly have gotten more out of the opportunity than the narrator and the woman he's dangling with. The whole point of "The Dangling Conversation" is for Simon to sound smart and poetic, so he drops names and hopes he accumulates some of the power of those whose names he uses for rhymes. He lists poets who happened to be hip at the time (Emily Dickinson, Robert Frost), but the only thing those names do is fill out the meter: he's not singing about them, just listing them. He could just as easily mention Wallace Stevens or Rod McKuen. In "The Dangling Conversation," it makes no difference.

As if the conversation isn't enough to make you want to dangle Simon out of a high-floor apartment window, his descriptions are even more appalling. "We sit and drink our coffee/Couched in our indifference/Like shells upon the shore," Simon sings. His point is to sound smart, sensitive: i.e., a good catch. But his overenunciated delivery (augmented by strings that seem to have wandered in from a different studio) also says, "Look how cool I am that I live this life of the mind. I am so, so smart." Simon didn't invent folk rock, as some have claimed: he invented elitist rock, and he carries its standard to this day.

THE GUESS WHO
"American Woman"
RCA, 1970

highest chart position: number one (three weeks)

One of the weirdest and most wonderful things about the Band was that it took a bunch of Canadians (save Levon Helm, their Arkansan secret weapon) to get at the heart of innumerable American pop forms and myths. The Guess Who are the Anti-Band. These north-of-the-border men picked up virtually every aspect of sixties rock they could scavenge—from heavy guitar to simpleminded, finger-pointing protest lyrics—but they could never put the sundry pieces together. Lead guitarist Randy Bachman eventually found in Bachman-Turner Overdrive a more appropriate context for his tendency to rock out in a simple way, but in the Guess Who such predilections were more than offset by the group's addiction to putting too many slim ideas into each song, ideas unworthy to carry a single verse—even when you add them up.

Bachman's foil in the Guess Who was Burton Cummings, one of those smarty-pants singer-pianists who was certain his talents ranged far beyond mere rock and roll. His own subsequent solo career was far more futile than Bachman's: by 1977 (the year of punk) he was reduced to writing "My Own Way to Rock" and singing it as if that way led directly to an Off-Off-Broadway theater. Bachman left BTO around the same time, leading to the first of many progressively more embarrassing Guess Who reunions (there was even a BTO revival). The music the Guess Who made during their intermittent cash-ins was appalling, almost bad enough to make one forget that they were insufferable the first time out.

Their most outrageously wrongheaded single during that first tour of duty was "American Woman." By 1970, criticism of the American government in a pop song had become old hat (although with troop levels in Vietnam still rising, it was far from inappropriate). But that was the only hat at the store when the Guess Who went shopping, so they tried to make it fit.

The song kicks off with a stuttering Bachman guitar line that's inviting enough until—by the second or second thousandth time he plays it—it starts inviting comparisons to Led Zeppelin's "Whole Lotta Love." Zep's riff, in turn, had been swiped off many of the songs Willie Dixon wrote in the late 1950s, but don't expect these genius critics of American culture to know that. We'll take first-generation derivativeness over second-generation any day.

"American Woman" stumbles because the lyrics use the Statue of Liberty as a symbol of what's wrong with America. Not necessarily a bad conceit (although don't forget that heavy rock can't stay away from sexism for too long), but Cummings sings "American woman/Stay away from me/American woman/Mama, let me be" like he's trying to dump a groupie. You don't believe any of the arguments he makes in the song, because he never lets you forget that he's a rock star. To heighten the Led Zeppelin wanna-be connection, Cummings holds the last syllable of some lines too long in a blatant Robert Plant imitation.

What undermines Cummings's performance most are the absurd ideas that come out of his mouth. He tells the U.S. babe "I've got more important things to do/Than spend my time growing old with you." Wait a minute: wasn't one aim of ending the war to give a generation of kids a chance to grow old in the shadow of the big lady in green? By the last verse he's singing, "American woman/Now get away" (hasn't she had enough of this already?), and then orders, "American woman/Listen what I say." Forget the internal contradiction: that last couplet is the point of the song. We hate everything you stand for, the Guess Who shout. Now will you please buy our record?

BLOODROCK
"D.O.A."
Capitol, 1971
highest chart position: number thirty-nine

In this wide world, there is much without a rational explanation. Why have so many planes and boats disappeared in the Bermuda Triangle? Who was Jack the Ripper? How come Tom Cruise gets to make movies with real actors like Paul Newman, Dustin Hoffman, and Robert Duvall? In the world of rock and roll, there are similarly inexplicable occurrences. Like, what possessed the members of the Texas group Bloodrock to write and record a song like "D.O.A."? Who at Capitol Records thought it could be a hit single? Finally, why did the public prove them right?

Even for a form of music suffused with songs about death, "D.O.A." is a milestone. This is undoubtedly the most gruesome, most graphic, and sickest song ever to hit the Top Forty.

Behind a two-note organ riff simulating an ambulance siren, the narrator of "D.O.A." (lead singer Jim Rutledge) describes in great detail his condition after having been in an airplane crash. He's in bad shape. Mere generalities about pain in his back and "something warm" flowing down his fingers only begin to paint this picture. "I try to move my arm and there's no feeling," he sings. "And when I look, I see there's nothing there." Just in case he had an inkling that his prognosis might not be hopeless, he hears the ambulance attendant say "there's no chance" for him.

His girlfriend, riding next to him, is beyond the no-chance stage. If this were a typical teen tragedy song, we'd be getting ready for the inevitable happy reunion in the afterlife (as in the Everly Brothers' "Ebony Eyes"), but by 1971 the rock audience was too sophisticated for that. Besides, this guy is far too interested in going on about himself. "Life is flowing out my body...The sheets are red and moist where I'm lying." For someone about to buy the farm, he's pretty vivid with his descriptions. In fact, he doesn't even sound like he's dying. He sounds like just another bored rock singer obsessed with himself.

As if the lyrics and the unbelievable vocals weren't bad enough, the song ends with Bloodrock stumbling and thumping to a close, symbolizing the narrator's stopping heartbeat as a siren wails into the distance. Fortunately, we didn't have to follow that siren, as "D.O.A." was Bloodrock's only Top Forty hit. We don't want to contemplate what the follow-up could have been.

HURRICANE SMITH
"Oh Babe, What Would You Say?"
Capitol, 1972
highest chart position: number three

The Peter Principle, as conceived by Dr.
Laurence Peter, states that sooner or later in professional life everyone
rises to his or her level of incompetence. Each time you do a job well
(or don't screw up), you get a promotion. If this progression continues
long enough, you will eventually be promoted into a job beyond your
abilities. Norman "Hurricane" Smith is the music industry's contribution to the Peter Principle.

Smith started out as a recording engineer for EMI studios in London.
As such, he happened to set up the microphones and twirl various
knobs as George Martin told him to during the Beatles' early sessions.
Having proved adept at these tasks (that is, he didn't accidentally erase
any tapes or mike an air-conditioner vent), Smith graduated to the role
of producer, working most noticeably on the early albums by British
head-music specialists Pink Floyd.

In the record business, after you've proved yourself competent on one
side of the glass, someone equally bankrupt of ideas will suggest that
you work on the other side. (In fairness, this career path is not
restricted to the record industry. How else can you explain Jon Peters
going from hairdreser to film producer to head of a Hollywood studio?)
So Norman changed his name to Hurricane and embarked on a new
career. Smith produced, arranged, conducted, and sang on this attempt
to grab the limelight for himself. As it turns out, "Hurricane" was an
apt moniker, since "Oh Babe, What Would You Say?" destroys all in its
path, especially your appetite.

Backed by a honking saxophone that evokes images of a goose being
tortured and a drippingly sweet string arrangement designed to
overcompensate for the sour vocal, this goofy, ersatz music-hall ditty is
more successful as Dada than as pop. The way Smith's voice breaks as
he tries to reach the high notes in the song's title line is perversely
sublime. So what if the guy's voice is as flat as Salisbury Plain? We can
only dream—with something resembling the thrill of jumping off a
cliff—what could have been if Smith had teamed up with the Shaggs.

We have to assume that Smith realized how ludicrous this record
sounded. Even hanging out with Pink Floyd couldn't have warped him
to the extent that he thought this was good. We will further assume
that Americans turned "Oh Babe, What Would You Say?" into a hit
because it is so appealingly bad. However, we're not willing to go so far
as to claim that the British bought this record for the same reason.
We're willing to bet that they actually liked it.

ROD STEWART
"Da Ya Think I'm Sexy?"
Warner Brothers, 1978
highest chart position: number one (four weeks)

Once upon a time, Rod Stewart didn't have to ask whether we thought he was sexy. In the early seventies, Stewart was that rare superstar whose commitment to his music rivaled his yearning for stardom. His first four solo albums (*The Rod Stewart Album, Gasoline Alley, Every Picture Tells a Story, Never a Dull Moment*) are among the most empathetic and open hearted of rock discs. No one as gifted as he could fail to arouse us. (By the way, as a four-disk set of essential rock and roll, these recordings annihilate his 1989 *Storyteller* anthology.)

Wanting to be a rock star is fine, but Stewart became a huckster, attracting millions of casual fans while repelling early admirers. What's most frustrating about his work since the mid-seventies is that he still has the talent but rarely indulges it. Stewart can still perform with pure soul if he works up even minimal enthusiasm—his 1985 rendition of Curtis Mayfield's "People Get Ready" is definitive—but most of the time he can't be bothered. Hence we are usually treated to something like "Love Touch," a slab of bland pop that deserved to be associated with the Redford/Winger/Hannah monstrosity *Legal Eagles*. He's gone from teddy boy to teddy bear.

Stewart's most cynical move to curry fleeting musical favor was "Da Ya Think I'm Sexy?" Like many pop stars in their second decade on the scene, Stewart in 1978 was a subject of attack on two sides. Punks reviled him because he had let his talents ossify; another new group of pop fans dismissed Stewart because he couldn't make them dance. Stewart would never consider trying to satisfy the punks, whose ruffian ways must have made the former Rod the Mod shudder, but the dance crowd—the much larger, more profitable market—that was something to tap into.

"Da Ya Think I'm Sexy?" was unlike other disco moves of the time by seasoned Brits (the Rolling Stones' resilient "Miss You," the Kinks' feeble "Superman") in that it was a complete break from Stewart's other work. Instead of being an evolutionary move with some logical rationale (the Stones, for example, were always on the prowl for new rhythms), "Da Ya Think I'm Sexy?" was a crass grab for a place in the new pop world. If disco was going to be what sold, Rod wanted to be part of it.

Stewart could not possibly have fashioned a lamer entry in the disco sweepstakes. He wrote the song with noted bad drummer Carmine Appice (who couldn't keep time for his former employers Vanilla Fudge and Jeff Beck), a warning to the listener that the beat would waver as soon as Carmine looked away from his metronome. The wobbly beat has all the thud of disco (sounding like a drum machine running out of batteries), and the simple synthesizer lead line is as annoying as a loudmouth barroom drunk on the stool next to you.

In such a setting the lyrics of "Da Ya Think I'm Sexy?" unfold. It's a pickup tale that ends in the inevitable one-night stand. Stewart can be interesting even at his worst, so there are a few throwaway lines of momentary honesty here, but every word he sings is undermined by his delivery. Stewart sings this song as if he's having a few drinks with the boys and boasting about his latest conquest. There's none of his trademark empathy, none of his attention to detail. There's nothing here to make us believe that he believes what he's singing. Like most boys' sexual boasts, "Da Ya Think I'm Sexy?" is a lie.

GRAND FUNK RAILROAD
"The Loco-Motion"
Capitol, 1974
highest chart position: number one (two weeks)

In many ways, Grand Funk Railroad is the prototypical heavy-metal band. In addition to having the requisite stupid name, the group churned out rock and roll at brain-splitting sound levels (eventually affecting their own), were universally hated by the critics, and were loved (almost as universally) by legions of kids who bought anything with their name on it. Their most lasting contribution was the inauguration of a practice that every heavy-metal band worthy of its blow dryers—from Van Halen ("Oh, Pretty Woman") to Great White ("Once Bitten, Twice Shy")—has found to be a fail-safe way to make it onto the charts: if you can't come up with an original tune good enough to put out as a single, bludgeon an instantly recognizable oldie.

This was a step Grand Funk Railroad had to make to secure chart domination. After four years of sold-out concerts and platinum albums, the trio scored their first major hit single in 1973 with "We're an American Band," a declaration of heavy-metal populism, a stance that similar groups have since exploited with similar success. Their follow-up single barely snuck into the Top Twenty, so the band decided to fall back on a surefire seller. After all, the First Law of Cover Versions is, if pop fans bought something once, they're primed to buy it again.

"The Loco-Motion," originally done by Little Eva, was the perfect choice. It topped the charts in 1962, and it was the kind of song that everybody knew—even people who had never heard it before. Best of all, although the song had sunk into the collective pop subconscious, it had been a hit so long ago that few of Grand Funk Railroad's core audience would distinctly remember the original. Not only was the band's audience not exactly a bunch of rock-and-roll historians, but many of them weren't yet conceived when the original version was.

Everything that was persuasive about the original "Loco-Motion" is missing here: charm, subtlety, wit, exuberance. Guitarist Mark Farner and company stumble their way through what had previously been recognized as a top-rank rock-and-roll dance song. They drag it along with ham-fisted power chords and a turgid back beat so inappropriate it's almost impossible to move to unless you happen to be Franken-stein's monster. And Grand Funk Railroad was never a band to overestimate the intelligence of its audience. In case a line like "a chug-a-lug motion like a railroad train" wasn't picturesque enough to explain what was going on, the band made train noises in the background. Thanks for clearing that up, guys.

Heavy-mental bands were not the only ones to rip off this lesson from rip-off masters Grand Funk Railroad. In 1988 an insubstantial Australian actress-turned-singer named Kylie Minogue sensed the need for a big hit to put her over to the American audience. She too recorded an instantly recognizable oldie guaranteed to land her a hit. Her frothy version of "The Loco-Motion" reached number three. We wonder how many people who bought it thought it was a cool cover of a Grand Funk Railroad song.

MELANIE
"Ruby Tuesday"
Buddah, 1970
highest chart position: number fifty-two

MELANIE
"Brand New Key"
Neighborhood, 1971
highest chart position: number one (three weeks)

Whenever people who weren't around at the time go on and on about how the Woodstock generation inspired uniformly magnificent music, we point them toward these two singles and stick cotton in our ears. Melanie, a folkish singer so wispy she made Donovan sound like Iron Butterfly, performed at Woodstock and was moved (by the mud? by Peter Townshend bashing Abbie Hoffman's head with a guitar? by the spiked punch?) to write "Lay Down (Candles in the Rain)," a mush-headed appeal for generational solidarity that was notable for being even more naive than most of the other mush-headed appeals for generational solidarity that were being written at the time. When the film *Woodstock* was shown in theaters, ticket-holders were encouraged to light candles as a sign of togetherness (or something like that) with the mud-drenched masses on the screen. "Lay Down (Candles in the Rain)" immediately established Melanie as a major force of bad music.

She promptly got worse. After trivializing Woodstock (which, to be fair, is an event that invites at least some trivialization, Joni Mitchell notwithstanding), she went after the Rolling Stones. Her version of "Ruby Tuesday" is so overdramatic and clumsy, it's easy to wonder if her role model for this recording wasn't Mick Jagger or even Marianne Faithfull but Sebastian Cabot circa *Sebastian Cabot, actor. Bob Dylan, poet.* Throughout the overwrought performance, Melanie inserts extra syllables and vocal flourishes in a desperate attempt to stamp her own imprint on the song. She sings a straightforward lyric like "She comes and then she goes" as if she had spent years agonizing over it. By furiously revving up the baroque melodrama when she gets to the song's fast sections, she blows what little power is to be gained from the speeding tempo. At such moments she sounds like she's gargling. When she finally gets to the clincher line, "You will lose your mind," it's easy to wonder if she's warning us of the dangers of repeatedly listening to her version of "Ruby Tuesday."

Then she got even worse. With the smash hit "Brand New Key," Melanie went for the lowest common denominator of pop singles: the juvenile double entendre. "I've got a brand-new pair of roller skates/ You've got a brand-new key" works as an innocent playground ditty, but it's clear what our hippier-than-we auteur is, er, slipping in through the back door. We usually only get to hear double entendres of such finesse at midnight showings of *The Rocky Horror Picture Show*. The song's arrangement is sugarless bubble gum, Melanie warbling across keys, unable to find any entrance into the song. To fellow hipsters this haphazard singing was taken to stand for ironic distance from the song. "Don't worry about the silly words," she seemed to say in her singing. "I'm above all that." The rock audience quickly tired of the novelty; after this chart-topper, Melanie never again had a Top Thirty single. On the flip side of "Brand New Key," Melanie noted, "Some say I got devil/Some say I got angel." Guess which got our vote.

ERIC CLAPTON
"Wonderful Tonight"
RSO, 1978
highest chart position: number sixteen

We're fans of guitarist-singer Eric Clapton, especially his blues side. We buy his argument that his turn from the raw blues of Cream and Derek and the Dominoes to sweet pop rock was emblematic of the inner peace he had finally been able to achieve after years of drug and personal problems. Fine by us. We'd rather have Clapton soft and alive than hard and dead. But no drug-recovery program forces its clients to get this soft. Slowhand should never be this slow.

"It's late in the evening," Clapton begins singing. We believe him, because thanks to the lulling guitar introduction we've already started to fall asleep. He slumps into a contrived devotional love song that has since found much usefulness as a high-school prom theme, which should give you a sense of how maudlin it is.

Yet even the devotion here is off. (Of course, Clapton has always been of two minds about some women. Ask George Harrison.) She makes him feel "wonderful tonight," but the most loving compliment he can offer her is that she looks "wonderful tonight." Wow, what a wise man. And another thing: what about last night, Eric? Did she look like dirt? We're certainly not going to ask about tomorrow morning.

Clapton snoozed through this performance all the way into the Top Twenty; perhaps he was saving his strength for future beer-sponsorship-deal negotiations. "Oh, my Michelob/You taste wonderful tonight."

BONNIE TYLER
"Faster Than the Speed of Night"
Columbia, 1983
highest chart position: did not chart

Some one-hit wonders will do anything for another shot. When singer Bonnie Tyler scored her number-three smash "It's a Heartache" in 1978, she immediately seemed primed for one-hit oblivion. Her singing style (caused partially by a 1976 throat operation) went out of its way to ape Rod Stewart's primal rasp; she seemed nothing more than a slightly talented clone jumping on a true original's bandwagon. None of her follow-up singles charted, and it seemed that was that.

But five years later Tyler hooked up with another second-tier one-hit rocker trying to pump some life into a dying career. Songwriter and producer Jim Steinman had also enjoyed tremendous success in 1978 as the musically flatulent Geppetto behind Meat Loaf's inexplicably multiplatinum *Bat Out of Hell* LP. His barrage of lengthy declamations, stolen Springsteen riffs (whose existence was not excused by the presence of several E Streeters on the record), and adolescent double entendres made Meat Loaf a massive star and Steinman an instant millionaire. Then the roof fell in.

Mr. Loaf (as the *New York Times* called him) blew out his voice on tour and couldn't record a follow-up for years. Frustrated by Meat's debilitation and envious that he wasn't yet a star in his own right, Steinman took the songs planned for the next Meat Loaf record, yelled them himself, and talked the folks at Epic into releasing it. The resulting album, *Bad for Good*, was such an over-the-top disaster that neither Steinman's nor, by association, Meat Loaf's career ever recovered. By 1983, both Tyler and Steinman were at the end of their respective ropes.

Tyler was desperate and willing to try anything new, even if it meant succumbing to Steinman's least grounded ideas ever. Their album together, *Faster Than the Speed of Night*, coupled Tyler's gruff tenor with Steinman songs that were so far out of her range she would have needed another operation to capture them. The album delivered a hit in "Total Eclipse of the Heart," a typically random Steinman image (what, we ask, is a partial eclipse of the heart?) that has no relation to any of the other lyrics in the song.

The deadliest cut on the disc was its title-track single. On it, Tyler is swamped by an enormous arrangement that sounds like every musician in the New York local took a turn adding clutter to the mix. Steinman's arrangements always squeeze too many instruments into too little space, but here there's so much nonsense that there's no place left to put the song. Tyler gives up when confronted with lines like, "You're such a pretty boy/Let me show you what to do and you'll do it/But you gotta move faster than the speed of night." Faster than the speed of night, Jim? What if we only move as fast as the speed of night? Will that be fast enough to escape this song?

RICHARD SIMMONS
"This Time"
Elektra, 1982
highest chart position: did not chart *anywhere*

During the aerobics craze of the early eighties, Richard Simmons represented the new breed of television huckster. Although televised religious ministries were stronger than ever thanks to the likes of Oral Roberts, Jimmy Swaggart, Jim and Tammy Faye Bakker, Jerry Falwell, and other current and future convicts, Simmons tapped into a want more deeply rooted in the American psyche than the desire for spiritual fulfillment: the quest for beauty. Face it, as much as people may talk about exercising for health reasons, the vast majority are doing it in the hopes that losing a few pounds will make them look more like Jane Fonda. (That's why you rarely see guys getting into aerobics; the only role model we have is Simmons.)

In addition to hosting his own exercise program, Simmons would pop up on any other show that would have him, from "The Regis Philbin Show" to "Hollywood Squares." That's not a real wide spectrum of programming, but it gives you an idea of who would have him. Not content with conducting a personal blitz against one medium, Simmons turned his attention to the flowering field of aerobics records: people put these albums on their home stereos and then work up a sweat moving the furniture in their living rooms around so they have enough space to do the workouts the leader barks from the vinyl haven. Aside from being put through your paces by a disembodied voice (did you ever think of what would happen if the record skipped? you'd be stuck trying to lift your rear end above your eyebrows), aerobics albums allowed the workouts to be backed up with a musical soundtrack to keep folks moving along with the rhythm. Most used an anonymous studio band; in special cases, tracks by name performers were pressed into service. However, when some motor-mouthed egomaniacs were involved, the star would not only program the workout but also be involved in the songs behind the exercises. Hence Simmons's entry into the field, *Reach*.

"This Time" was Simmons's grope for a hit single. "You must do it for you this time./No one means more than you this time," Simmons (who obviously has no need for grammar) squeaks his philosophy of self-love over the opening strains of heavily synthesized orchestration. Addressing his audience of overweight, no-self-esteem followers, he flatly intones his fuzzy paradigms of feel-good pop psychology: "You can love

RICHARD SIMMONS

THIS TIME
b/w
REACH

From the
album
"Reach"

the hurt away…'cause in your heart you're here to stay," and "You must think with your heart this time./Don't you know that for every change there might be pain inside you?" (Uh-oh, he's getting mighty close to Leo Buscaglia territory.) The music has the slightly anthemic quality that theme songs inevitably blast, ending with a swelling of synthesized strings and cymbal rolls that sound like fighter jets strafing the studio (we can only hope orders were to take no prisoners). Worst of all, the beat is far too slow to serve as a soundtrack for doing aerobics, the ostensible purpose of this whole stupid enterprise.

After *Reach* dropped from the charts, Simmons put out an exercise video that featured him working out with the relatives of famous people—Sylvester Stallone's mother, John Travolta's father. We're still not sure who was doing the slumming.

CAT STEVENS
"Moon Shadow"
A&M, 1971
highest chart position: number thirty

Before he became everybody's favorite book critic, Steven Georgiou made an extremely good living writing and singing songs that expressed the emotional depth and philosophy of breathy sixth-grade girls. In a career studded with annoying songs ("Peace Train," "Morning Has Broken," "Oh Very Young"—admit it, you know 'em all), "Moon Shadow" stands out as a crowning achievement. It epitomizes the hazy outlook of Stevens, his audience, and the most successful early seventies pop. Against a background of acoustic guitar, simple tambourine, and soft backing vocals (just perfect for the audience sing-along portion of the local opening act when Brewer and Shipley came to campus), "Moon Shadow" reflected the postprotest, let's-make-the-best-of-a-bad-situation sentiment after Kent State showed that trying to change the situation could get you killed.

Stevens sings of a series of hypothetical misfortunes, each involving the loss of a body part (basically a listing of Muslim punishments less cruel than the one he'd later suggest for Salman Rushdie), and then comes up with a happy-go-lucky justification for not worrying about it. Hey, if he loses his hands, he'll never have to work again; if he goes blind, he won't have to cry; if he loses his mouth ("All my teeth/North and south"—not to mention those on the sides), he won't have to talk to anybody. (The joke here is far too obvious, so we'll just move along.)

Then there's the moon shadow itself. Why is it following Cat? Is it trying to cut off his arm? And if so, could the moon shadow make sure it's the one Cat uses to write down his lyrics?

THE HOLLIES
"Stop in the Name of Love"
Atlantic, 1983
highest chart position: number twenty-nine

PHIL COLLINS
"You Can't Hurry Love"
Atlantic, 1982
highest chart position: number ten

The Hollies started out as one of the innumerable "beat groups" that appeared in the wake of the Beatles' success. Time and again they climbed to the upper reaches of the British singles charts with covers of American rhythm-and-blues standards. Tunes such as "Searchin'" by the Coasters, "Stay" by Maurice Williams and the Zodiacs, and "Just One Look" by Doris Troy were homogenized in Hollies style, but they were still recognizable enough to be hits. Having established themselves in this way, the Hollies were given the chance to record material by some of England's best non-Beatle songwriters and even turned in some decent originals, like "King Midas in Reverse," that took advantage of their airy harmonies.

Twenty years and countless personnel changes after their first British hit, four members of the band's mid-sixties grouping (Allan Clarke, Graham Nash, Tony Hicks, and Bobby Elliott) reunited to produce one of the most abominable reunion albums of the eighties. Returning to their original method, the band released a cover version of an American R&B classic as a single: the Supremes' inarguable "Stop! In the Name of Love." The Hollies' rendition was called "Stop in the Name of Love." The missing exclamation point tells much of the story.

Like almost all of the great Motown hits built around bassist James Jamerson and drummer Benny Benjamin, the Supremes' "Stop! In the Name of Love" is as astonishing a recording as it is a composition. Not a note is wasted; even a cursory listen reveals that everyone in the studio is deeply connected with the song. It's the kind of record that makes something as seemingly inconsequential as a three-minute pop song so important to millions.

But the Hollies' interpretation is all about distance. The antiseptic production makes you wonder if any two instruments or voices were recorded in the same studio (forget at the same time). The producers here are listed as the Hollies, Graham Nash (wait: isn't he supposedly a member of the Hollies?), Stanley Johnston, and Paul Bliss. That adds up to six producers (unless we're supposed to count Nash twice), enough to field a hockey team. It sounds as if they passed tapes back and forth, each responsible for a different overdub. Most embarrassing is Tony Hicks's inappropriate screeching guitar solo, which sounds like it was left over from another song and accidentally dropped into the mix by one of the plethora of producers. It would have helped the performance if at least two of the six overseers had discussed it; the dragging arrangement suggests that each *auteur* loaded his own luggage onto the song, oblivious to all the other packages, until the poor song couldn't move anymore.

The Hollies' "Stop in the Name of Love" was appalling, but at least they didn't intentionally belittle the Supremes classic, which seems to be the idea behind Phil Collins's disembowelment of "You Can't Hurry Love." The diminutive Genesis front man has always considered record making little more than an opportunity to mug for the microphones: nearly all of his "serious" tunes are forced, like Andrew Ridgeley's need for a solo career. Collins, in love with the idea of amiably disposable pop, conjures up a version of "You Can't Hurry Love" that is as soothing as the original was admonitory. The rhythm section captures the Jamerson/Benjamin sound without any of its yearning. Collins's multitracked vocals mean to be so cute you'll want to pinch his cheeks; instead they are so condescending and charmless you want to grab him by the throat. "You Can't Hurry Love" is a facile exercise for Collins, a simpleminded attempt to prove that through studio wizardry he can recreate a particular sound. But there is no indication that he cares about the song. It sounds like he can't wait for the song to end so he can practice smiling for the video.

JANIS IAN
"At Seventeen"
Columbia, 1975
highest chart position: number three

Janis Ian represents the "feel my pain" school of rock songwriting. In 1967, at the age of sixteen, Ian hit the pop charts with "Society's Child," the tale of a white girl and her black boyfriend who must break off their relationship because people—you guessed it—just don't understand. After Ian was featured on the television special "Inside Pop: The Rock Revolution," hosted by noted rock-and-roll wild man Leonard Bernstein, "Society's Child" raced up the charts, in the process getting banned in some sections of the country, being championed by its supporters as "socially relevant" (nobody ever said it was any good as a song), and inspiring more bad high-school English compositions that year than even "A Day in the Life."

In 1975, by which time we had gotten used to her having been a one-hit wonder, Ian showed up again, this time with another angst-filled look at the problems of pubescent youth. "At Seventeen" chronicles the loneliness and desperation of every teenager who ever sat home on a Saturday night, sure that everybody else was out having a great time (and probably making fun of you to boot). These are feelings that every teenager has at some point; the problem with this song is that they are presented in terms so self-pitying that it's no surprise nobody wanted to hang out with her. "The valentines I never knew/The Friday night charades of youth/Were spent on one more beautiful." Definite image problem. Janis, did you ever stop to think that the reason you weren't picked for the basketball team might not have had anything to do with your pimples? Maybe if you stopped whining about valentines and started concentrating on your perimeter shot, you'd have a better chance. (Also, as many have pointed out, Ian was short.)

Even more stupefying, the basic concept of the song is a typical teenage revenge fantasy. "Their small-town eyes will gape at you/In dull surprise when payment due/Exceeds accounts received/At seventeen," Ian sings in her best someday-I'll-be-big-and-important-and-then-I'll-show-you whimper.

After Janis got this off her chest she had nothing else to say and promptly disappeared again. (Cross your fingers.)

BARRY MCGUIRE
"Eve of Destruction"
Dunhill, 1965
highest chart position: number one (one week)

THE SPOKESMEN
"Dawn of Correction"
Decca, 1965
highest chart position: number thirty-six

Barry McGuire began his recording career as a member of the New Christy Minstrels, a group of early-sixties folkies whose members at one time or another included Gene Clark of the Byrds, Kenny Rogers and most of the members of the First Edition, and a young man from Detroit named Vincent Furnier, who later changed his name to Alice Cooper. (OK, Alice Cooper wasn't one of the New Christy Minstrels. We just wanted to make sure you were still paying attention.)

In 1965, McGuire enjoyed his first and only major hit, although listening to "Eve of Destruction" you get the impression that he wasn't capable of enjoying very much. "Eve of Destruction" is a pointed rail against the social and political climate of the time, building from acoustic guitar and muffled drums intended to sound like distant artillery fire. McGuire goes beyond Dylan in asking why things are wrong and underlining that things don't have to be this way: "Eve of Destruction" is so bereft of hope, McGuire suggests, we all might as well just pack it in now. From the Middle East to Communist China to Selma, Alabama (you can laugh, but *you* try to rhyme *China* and *Alabama*), McGuire sees everyone and everything as rotten. We're all hypocrites, he says, and we give thanks for the food on our tables while we hate our neighbors. By song's end, McGuire is a frustrated, paranoid mess, spitting out words in his best "Positively Fourth Street" imitation, waiting for the button to be pushed, but sounding completely unconvincing. McGuire has nihilistic punk antipolitics, but no punk energy. He's not angry; he's just petulant.

McGuire's nihilism alienated even many who bought "Eve of Destruction," so it wasn't surprising that an answer record, the first hit protest song about a hit protest song, appeared almost immediately. Hitting the charts just before "Eve of Destruction" peaked, "Dawn of Correction" was as opportunistic as most public radical-right gestures. It also paved the way for the far-right wacko hit of the following year, Sgt. Barry Sadler's pro-murder "Ballad of the Green Berets."

The words to "Dawn of Correction" don't pretend that everything is hunky-dory: it insists that listeners do everything they can to protect this nation from the ungodly Red menace or "there'll be no voting in future generations." This is also the only song of the sixties with a straight-faced endorsement of the concept of mutually assured destruction. "The buttons are there to ensure negotiation,/So don't be afraid, boy, it's our only salvation"? Did Pat Buchanan write this song under a pseudonym?

Actually, "Dawn of Correction" was penned by veteran songwriters John Madara and Dave White, who had previously come up with Danny and the Juniors' "At the Hop" and Lesley Gore's "You Don't Own Me." It's an unlikely trio of hit songs, and the track record suggests that the intensity of the answer song to "Eve of Destruction" lasted only as long as it took to write it.

HUEY LEWIS AND THE NEWS
"Hip to Be Square"
Chrysalis, 1986
highest chart position: number three

It makes sense that Huey Lewis and the News were one of the most popular bands of the eighties. Huey was good-looking in a dumb guy-next-door way, a rock-and-roll Dobie Gillis, and his band could appear to play hard even if they neglected to generate any intensity.

This San Francisco sextet was responsible for several empty-headed Top Ten hits—among them "I Want a New Drug," "The Heart of Rock and Roll," and "Stuck With You"—but those annoyances were merely bland compared to "Hip to Be Square," which was genuinely malevolent, popping up everywhere from college marching band halftime shows to Las Vegas showrooms. It was also big at weddings.

Musically, "Hip to Be Square" was marginally more interesting than what Lewis and company usually conjured up: the fast beat was agreeable enough and the band sounded less reined-in than usual by the group's inevitable drum-machine taskmaster. Lyrically, however, this was a perfect anthem of rationalization for uneasy sellouts. The narrator of the song has cut his hair, scored a "good" job, and realized that, yes, it's hip to be square, because in this context "square" means financially successful. I'm so square, la la la, where's the cash? (Where we come from, square means seventh-grade science teachers whose scalps are soaked in Brylcreem.) The song ends with the band and its frat-boy horn section shouting the title over and over like a beer commercial mantra. If we say it's hip to be square enough times, they think, people might believe us.

"Hip to Be Square" was a pox on rock and roll in the late eighties. People invoked the song ad nauseam, claiming it was hip to accept corporate sponsorship, respect Dan Quayle, or take that high-paying job at Dow Chemical. Underlying "Hip to Be Square" is the idea that nothing "hip" matters, so why worry about any of that? If Drexel Burnham Lambert had a P.A. system (before they had to install air-raid sirens), a Muzak version of "Hip to Be Square" would have played twenty-four hours a day.

ERIC CARMEN
"All by Myself"
Arista, 1975
highest chart position: number two

When he was with the Raspberries, Eric Carmen succeeded in writing and recording pop songs at a time when very few bands outside of the Kasenetz-Katz bubble-gum music operation were. Songs like "Go All the Way" and "Overnight Sensation (Hit Record)" sounded terrific over the radio, but Carmen's songs always seemed one shade brighter than "1-2-3, Red Light" or "Yummy, Yummy, Yummy." You had the feeling that if they had been recorded by someone else, these songs would have been indistinguishable from those of the 1910 Fruitgum Company. This point was proven when second-generation bubble-gum star Shaun Cassidy recorded Carmen's "That's Rock and Roll." The result may have been a hit record, but it was certainly not rock and roll.

After the Raspberries broke up in 1974, Carmen attempted to move away from singing for teenagers and break into the burgeoning field of "adult contemporary." This was music for people who grew up with rock and roll, considered it "their" music, but couldn't relate to the hit songs they were hearing on the radio. Because those people would rather have died than run the risk of sounding like their parents ("How can you listen to that crap?" was a standard refrain they grew up with), whole new market shares sprung up consisting of people looking for a more tonal music that they could listen to without feeling totally out of touch with the contemporary scene. Carmen's first solo single, "All by Myself," wasn't Rachmaninoff (who originated its main riff), but it sure comes close to being bubble-gum for adults. It had at least a tenuous connection with the more ballad-oriented side of soft rock, and it was drenched in self-pity. In the mid-seventies, that added up to money. (Go ask Clive Davis.)

"When I was young/I never needed anyone/And making love was just for fun./Those days are gone." The first four lines of the song tell us everything we need to know about the narrator, but unfortunately Carmen keeps singing. He feels so intensely sorry for himself that there's no reason for us to bother: he has it wrapped up. We want either to slap his face or to offer him some Prozac. We don't, however, want to offer him strings and a subclassical piano solo, but that's what our sad singer uses to accentuate his pain. As if that's not enough, Carmen hammers home "All by Myself" with bombastic drum parts that slam against the brain. These dramatic snare shots had a lasting presence: they set the pattern for Carmen's future labelmates, fellow self-pity specialists Air Supply.

The pop audience must have assumed Carmen got all his crying out of his system with "All by Myself": he didn't score another Top Ten single until 1987, when he coasted on the success of the film *Dirty Dancing* with "Hungry Eyes," a song title more appropriate for the title of a bad horror film. Last we saw him he was on the *Dirty Dancing* tour, wading between professional dry humpers.

THE ROLLING STONES
"Emotional Rescue"
Rolling Stones, 1980
highest chart position: number three

The Rolling Stones' 1980 album *Emotional Rescue* was a depressing return to middling seventies form (listened to *Goat's Head Soup* lately?) after the welcome aberration of 1978's *Some Girls*. There was little on *Emotional Rescue* that was flat-out awful, but much of it was filled with lazy throwaways—elemental jams that shouldn't have been considered worthy of release on a Rolling Stones record. (In fact, much of *Emotional Rescue* was outtakes from *Some Girls* and previous records.) The blues cut ("Down in the Hole") was distant, the rockers ("Summer Romance," "She's So Cold") were secondhand, Keith Richards's singing ("All about You") was irredeemably sleazy, and Mick Jagger's singing on a love ballad like "Indian Girl" was utterly unconvincing. They didn't care; why should we?

The least convincing track on *Emotional Rescue* was the ready-made title track. The frankly disco "Miss You" had been a number-one smash two years earlier, so the Stones, temporarily deprived of any interesting new ideas, felt they had no choice but to go to the well. But whereas "Miss You" was energetic and drew strength from being the group's first entry in a new genre, "Emotional Rescue" showed them succumbing to all the affectations of disco and invoking none of its heady strengths.

The dull, thudding beat of "Emotional Rescue" wastes Charlie Watts, but the track is merely boring until Jagger wanders in. Then it becomes a riot. His attempt at a falsetto, which leaves him somewhere between Sylvester the disco singer and Sylvester the cat, immediately transforms the song into camp. He may have pretensions to royalty, but as a falsetto warbler, the 1980 Jagger was no Prince. Nearly six minutes long in its LP version, "Emotional Rescue" is supposed to be a promise of redemption to a lady in love distress, but you can't hear Jagger's promises ("I'll be your savior/Steadfast and true") because you're laughing too hard. Perhaps Jagger sang this in falsetto as a dare; there's no other reason he would want to sound like the disco version of Alvin Chipmunk.

As if his falsetto weren't enough reason for us to hope Jagger comes down with laryngitis before the song ends, we have to deal with a spoken section. Stifling a laugh (he must have known this was ridiculous), Jagger intones, "Umm, yes, you could be mine. Tonight and every night. I will be your knight in shining armor coming to your emotional rescue." Soon he starts babbling like John Houseman about "riding across the desert/In a fine Arab charger," and all we can do is hope he gets stuck in the middle of the Sahara without food or water. (Also without Bobby Keys, whose saxophone playing on this track is the only part that isn't embarrassing.) The Rolling Stones had a rough time in the eighties, but never did they sound more out of it than they did on "Emotional Rescue."

HERMAN'S HERMITS
"I'm Henry VIII, I Am"
MGM, 1965
highest chart position: number one (one week)

When one perceives true talent, the first reaction is to look on with awe. For some, this is followed by a second reaction in which they try to figure out how they can get a piece of the action. When the Beatles appeared on "The Ed Sullivan Show" and touched off the British Invasion in 1964, they not only opened the gates for an infusion of great music but, like a ship docking in a harbor, they also dragged along with them every bit of garbage that got caught in their wake.

Herman's Hermits were formed as the Heartbeats in the first flush of the Beatles' British success. The band name was changed when a resemblance was noted between lead singer Peter Noone and the cartoon character Sherman from "The Bullwinkle Show." (Yeah, we know, why not Sherman's Shermits?) After the Fab Four broke through in the States, record labels—suddenly enamored of all things British—started searching for their very own mop-tops to make the girls squeal and help fill the company coffers. Herman's Hermits were snapped up by MGM Records (spin away, Hank Williams). Financially it was a great move: with their first seventeen singles they scored eighteen Top Forty hits ("There's a Kind of Hush" and "No Milk Today" was a double-sided hit). Musically, well...

Instead of experimenting as the Beatles did at all phases of their career, Herman's Hermits hit their mark from the very beginning and continued to hit it until they pounded it into the ground. Producer Mickie Most chose material for the group that would play off the youthful (read: dumb) exuberance of Noone and hearken back to the days of British music-hall entertainment in an effort to appeal to those under the age of ten and over the age of senility. "I'm Henry VIII, I Am" is slightly more tuneful than another song that demands a democratic revolution, Napoleon XIV's "They're Coming to Take Me Away, Ha-Haaa!" That, and the fact that the Ramones nicked the "second verse/same as the first" couplet from the Hermies, is all we can say for it.

We can, however, say lots against it. It trivialized Beatles rock into the sort of cavalier music-hall nonsense it was supposed to displace. Noone's attempts to imagine himself not as King Henry VIII but as the eighth loser who "married the widow next door" indicate that the tired woman must have had something about the name Henry, because there's no other reason anyone would want to spend time with this singer. Isn't the singer worried about what happened to Henrys I, II, III, IV, V, VI, and VII? Of course not: he's a British music-hall twit who doesn't have a brain. La la la.

Drummer Barry Whitham carries off a passable Pete Best impersonation, and the guitar solo (by either Derek Leckenby or Keith Hopwood—or maybe Jimmy Page was short on cash that week and would do a session for anybody) hints that this might have some tenuous connection to rock, but—boom!—Peter blunders back in and it's a joke again. For Noone, music is all arbitrary whimsy. Care about the words I'm singing? he asks. Never thought of that. La la la.

STEPHEN STILLS
"Love the One You're With"
Atlantic, 1970
highest chart position: number fourteen

"Love the One You're With" exemplifies the smug stupidity that defines West Coast rock in general and the Crosby, Stills, and Nash axis of it in particular. Here, in a nutshell, is the clearest reason to despise all that tripe.

"Love the One You're With" was recorded during one of Stills's periodic solo spells. These forays are always caused by Steve's frustration that he's not being given enough room to embarrass himself in a group context, and they are always followed by a cash-infusion reunion of one group or another. This single appeared on his debut album (with the expected megalomaniacal, homonymous title), which included inexplicable appearances by Eric Clapton and Jimi Hendrix (unless you assume that they were too stoned to notice where they were).

The rhythm of "Love the One You're With" is in the upbeat Youngbloods mode, with enough high-in-the-mix acoustic guitar playing to cloak his fetid lead guitar rhythms. The lyrics have long been taken to celebrate communal ecstasy (groovy, man), but in fact they are so sexually selfish it's easy to see why Stills hung around with David Crosby.

The lyrics pivot around the rancid chorus line, "If you can't be with the one you love, honey, love the one you're with." What Stills is really saying is that if you're a young rock musician on the road (Stills's career resounds with proof that he can't write from a point of view other than his immediate one) and your current "old lady" doesn't happen to be in the same room as you this very moment, feel free to jump on the first G.T.O. you see. Go on, it's cool. In other words, for Stills the whole point of the sexual revolution was to give him more freedom to be a jerk. Right on?

THE KNACK
"Good Girls Don't"
Capitol, 1979
highest chart position: number eleven

THE KNACK
"Baby Talks Dirty"
Capitol, 1980
highest chart position: number thirty-eight

These days we can hardly remember the Knack, even if they have reunited. They appeared out of nowhere, pretended to be the Beatles, treated their audience like shit, begged for forgiveness, didn't get it, and disappeared. But only a moment's hearing reminds us how "Good Girls Don't" and "Baby Talks Dirty" ruined our day every time we accidentally punched them up on the car radio.

Just when we thought we had washed the smell of "My Sharona," the group's number-one debut single, out of our clothes and our minds, the follow-up single, "Good Girls Don't," left us hip-deep in garbage all over again.

"Good Girls Don't" bothered us for all the same reasons as "My Sharona"—snide lyrics, smug vocals, messy drumming, guitar lines ripped off from every British Invasion band you can think of (we're thinking of Herman's Hermits)—but "Good Girls Don't" added a veneer of vicious sexism so thick that even the combined forces of Andrew Dice Clay, Sam Kinison, and most of the people who vote regularly for Jesse Helms couldn't cut through it. The peppy music was a Beatles rip-off, but the words were 2 Live Crew. The chorus ("Good girls don't/Good girls don't/Good girl don't/But I do") doesn't merely give life to a fourteen-year-old boy's sex fantasy à la the Bangles' "In My Room." Instead, this song is about singer Doug Fieger's hatred of any groupie who won't bend down to his every demand. The way he sings indicates that if you're a good girl, you're a piece of trash. You can buy his records, of course, but don't come near him.

"Good Girls Don't" caused a bit of controversy with one line, "When she's sittin' on your face," which the band rerecorded as "When she puts you in your place" in the single version. Aside from indicating that the band didn't have the courage to stand up for their music (no surprise), the new line suggests a whole new action for the non–good girl in the song, namely knee Fieger in the balls and run.

The Knack paused briefly from smirking and counting their money to record the album ...*But the Little Girls Understand*, the title of which recalled the Doors—whom the Knack hoped to replace as L.A.'s finest—more than Howlin' Wolf (the original source). Having used up both of their feeble ideas on their debut album (and even that had

64

covers, namely an automatic version of Buddy Holly's "Heartbeat"), they rewrote some of the debut's songs and hoped that their core audience of little girls would understand. (The misogynist album title can be taken to mean that although anyone with a mature brain hates them—even critics—prepubescent girls will accept anything.) The most obvious and deplorable remake on ...*But the Little Girls Understand* was "Baby Talks Dirty," a retread of the already derivative beat and chord changes of "My Sharona." By then, though, the joke had worn thin, the little girls had wised up and gone elsewhere, and the song barely scraped into the Top Forty. The only people talking dirty to the Knack now were their former fans.

MIKE + THE MECHANICS
"The Living Years"
Atlantic, 1989
highest chart position: number one (one week)

After Peter Gabriel skedaddled in 1975, Genesis wasn't all the fault of Phil Collins. The reason the drummer and replacement front man needed a solo career, after all, was to have more room. Among boring rock trios, only Beck, Bogert, and Appice and Emerson, Lake, and Palmer were more confining to its members. Collins's bandmates in the dwindling unit, guitarist Mike Rutherford and keyboardist Tony Banks, took advantage of the extra time their Live Aid-hogging comrade gave them. Banks wrote music that made some boring movies even more dreary and also formed Bankstatement, a band that never garnered enough interest to need one. Rutherford had more luck, joining with several other born sidemen to front Mike + the Mechanics.

Rutherford's foil in Mike + the Mechanics was Paul Carrack, a journeyman singer and keyboardist who appeared in many groups throughout the seventies and eighties and left a lasting imprint on none of them. He sang "How Long" for Ace and "Tempted" for Squeeze. In the eighties, Carrack was one of rock's most annoying utility infielders, inadequately filling in for sorely missed, departed stars. Eventually Carrack found himself in Rutherford's orbit and helped him turn Mike + the Mechanics into an airy pop unit that expanded upon the banal homilies of Genesis. Although you might have thought it impossible, the sound of Mike + the Mechanics is even more softheaded than that of Genesis; although Rutherford's guitar is supposedly the lead instrument, he's happy to submerge it under gallons of wishy-washy synthesizer and tentative drum-machine beats. We never thought we'd say this, but when we hear Mike + the Mechanics, we almost miss Phil Collins.

Carrack is Rutherford's mouthpiece (Mike doesn't sing), and in the title track to the Mechanics' *Living Years* LP, the guitarist gives him the sappiest lyric that ever confronted the hired hand. The idea behind "The Living Years" is simple and straightforward: a grown man mourns the death of his father and ponders why they weren't able to reach a rapprochement while the old man was still alive. It's not an original idea, but it is a notion that in the right hands can lend itself to some interesting permutations.

Not in these hands. With all the subtlety of a gown worn by Cher at the Academy Awards, Mike + the Mechanics turn this tale of self-pity (the lyrics are far more concerned with the narrator's feelings than anything the father might have felt) into a babbling mess. The lyric climaxes when the narrator notes that many of his dead father's features wound up in those of his grandson. Harry Chapin (relax, we'll get to him) is spinning in his grave.

As if the lyrics and the slick accompaniment weren't enough to ensure the inclusion of "The Living Years" here, Rutherford tries to hammer home the song with a manipulative method he probably picked up from *The Sound of Music*, a gimmick that has turned many a pop song into self-parody: a chorus of children who enunciate far too well. Such a move suggests that the band believed in the song so deeply that they felt a soothing children's chorus would add an intergenerational element or some nonsense like that. The children's chorus is merely a ploy to get the listener to feel something that the song doesn't convey on its own; even punks sometimes feel the hair on their arms stand on end when they hear a children's chorus. In "The Living Years," all the children's choir does is accentuate the by-the-numbers laziness of the song. It's so lackadaisical that when Carrack sings the word "living," you wonder if he's being ironic.

ANDREW GOLD
"Lonely Boy"
Asylum, 1977
highest chart position: number seven

It wasn't my fault!

Hollywood kids have it tough. No, really. Take Andrew Gold, for instance. His mom, Marni Nixon, was a singer (she gave Milli Vanilli role model Audrey Hepburn something to lip-synch to in *My Fair Lady*) and his father, Ernest Gold, wrote film soundtracks (*Exodus* for one). So Andrew was destined for a music career. He had his own bands and by his early twenties was escorting Linda Ronstadt and leading her band. If there was anything keeping Linda away from rocking out more than her manager and producer Peter Asher, it was Andrew. His precise arrangements undercut—

Wait. We're so sorry. We're making fun of poor, sensitive Andrew. And he has had it so hard in life. If you can stand it, you can find out about his travails by listening to his sole solo smash, "Lonely Boy." It tells the story of a sensitive young lad born in "the summer of '51," just like our Andy, and takes him to a time when he was eighteen and had to leave home. Gold sings the tale as if it is unique. Ask him, and he'll tell you nobody else in the history of the planet Earth ever felt the need to leave home when he or she was eighteen.

What was the trauma that made him "Oh, what a lonely boy"? Was he abused? Not that we can tell. Were there crippling financial problems at home? Nope. Did he have a dog named Foot Foot who was run over by a steamroller? Doesn't sound like it. No, Andrew had something much, much worse happen to him. We're going to tell you what it is, but our publisher's lawyers insist that we warn you that the next paragraph is so awful, so horrible, it might ruin your life almost as thoroughly as it did Andrew's. Are you ready?

He had a sister.

(We'll pause here for a moment to let you recover from the shock.)

That's it—and that's all. His sister never did anything bad to him, never detuned his piano, never took a hammer to his piggy bank. She simply...was. Listen, Goldie, even Marcel Proust wasn't this hypersensitive. Even Esau wasn't this pissed off at his younger sibling, and he had good reason. Andy whines on and on, blaming everything on her, although it doesn't sound like anything bad ever happened to him except her being born. Andy, grow up!

Oh yeah, the music. It's boring mid-seventies Asylum music that thinks it's rocking out because the drums are mixed a little louder.

HARRY CHAPIN
"Taxi"
Elektra, 1972
highest chart position: number twenty-four

HARRY CHAPIN
"Cat's in the Cradle"
Elektra, 1974
highest chart position: number one (one week)

From all accounts, Harry Chapin was a great man. He hated to turn down a request to play a benefit for a needy organization, devoted countless hours to worthy charities, and genuinely felt that one person could make a difference. When he died in a car crash on the Long Island Expressway in 1981 (while on his way to yet another benefit performance), many people were truly upset and, to be honest, we were also. Chapin seemed to be on the verge of actually writing a good song. After all the stuff he'd already put out, the odds were that he'd have to come up with one soon.

Chapin's shtick was the "story song"—sort of a short story with characters and setting and action and a moral, all set to music. The most important requirement of Chapin's genre, however, was to present the song in a highly strained and overworked manner that seemingly goes on forever. Rather than short stories, Chapin's songs more closely resemble the novels of Thomas Wolfe before editor Maxwell Perkins took to them with blue pencil and machete.

Chapin had his first major radio exposure with "Taxi," a six-minute-plus opus. The tale of a hack driver who picks up an old high-school girlfriend in his cab one night, "Taxi" stretched both the time limits of Top Forty radio and listeners' attention spans. By the time he drops her off and stuffs that twenty-dollar tip in his shirt, most of us have bailed out of the ride and walked the rest of the way. (And this narrator is so unrelentingly verbose that there's no way he'd pocket the Jackson silently, as he describes in the song. He'd force her to hear him declaim on the irony for at least two more verses.)

Two and a half years later Chapin had the biggest hit of his career with "Cat's in the Cradle." That mess begins with the birth of a boy and, although the father loves his son, he has a job that takes him out on the road, so he can't be around that much. The kid grows up and, like any other kid, wants to hang out with his dad, but dang it, Dad's just got too many important things to do. It's OK because the son understands and tells his friends that he wants to grow up to be just like Pop. More time passes; by now you worry that the kid's going to grow up to be a mass murderer, but Chapin already covered that angle in an earlier song, so instead we get a scene where the father calls up his son (now married with his own kids) to see if he can come over and spend a little time. I'd really like to, Dad, the son says, but the kids aren't feeling well and I really don't have the time right now. "And as I hung up the phone it occurred to me," the father sings, "my boy was just like me." Oooh, the irony of it all! Oooh, the social commentary! Oooh, the tidy sappiness!

At least by the end of "Cat's in the Cradle," Chapin's characters are attempting to talk to each other, which is more than can be said for the folks in Mike + the Mechanics' "The Living Years" and Andrew Gold's "Lonely Boy." Still, we can't help but feel that one of these songs was probably a favorite of every character in every John Hughes upper-middle-class—suburban-teendom-is-existential-terror film.

ANDY GIBB AND VICTORIA PRINCIPAL
"All I Have to Do Is Dream"
RSO, 1981
highest chart position: number fifty-one

Love makes us all do stupid things. Couples celebrate their love in ways that look foolish to the outside world. Far too often the desire to be close to a loved one can lead you to bring him or her into parts of your life that should remain separate.

When you're a celebrity, the possibilities for acting stupid in these ways increase exponentially. The romance between teenybopper idol Andy Gibb and nighttime-soap airhead Victoria Principal (Pamela Ewing on "Dallas") was big Hollywood news in the early eighties (it was especially big news to Gibb's press agents, who no longer had Top Ten singles to flog). It helped that the two lovebirds were agreeable. Their photographs were everywhere, accompanied by brief articles in which they swore their endless love. Alas, as with most Hollywood assertions of true love, this pair didn't last too long. (Fine by us; imagine the bland entertainer that could have resulted from that gene pool.) Heartbroken, Gibb didn't last much longer himself.

Yet one artifact remains from the affair: a duet single by Andy and Victoria, "All I Have to Do Is Dream." And all Victoria had to do was get voice lessons. At no point in this cover of the Everly Brothers classic did executive producer Gibb let his duet partner go it alone. He covered for her, as a lover should.

But Gibb himself doesn't have much to offer to the song. Aside from the novelty of hearing a Gibb brother warble along with someone who has an even higher voice, his vocal performance is far below even that of his hits "I Just Want to Be Your Anything" and "Shadow Dancing." Afraid of overshadowing Principal, he stays in the background: even his few solo sections are brief and deferential.

This is soft rock at its most squishy: weak drums provide no beat, mushy synthesized strings conjure up no atmosphere. All you hear in the vocals are one mediocre singer and his untalented girlfriend hamming up their few moments in the spotlight. If J.R. had any brains, he would have had someone follow Pamela to the studio and steal the master tapes to "All I Have to Do Is Dream," thus rescuing the Ewing family from unnecessary scandal. That would have been true love.

RICHARD HARRIS
"MacArthur Park"
Dunhill, 1968
highest chart position: number two

Jimmy Webb was one of the hottest song-
writers around during the late sixties. His tunes for Glen Campbell and
the Fifth Dimension (a black version of the Mamas and the Papas)
were not just smash hits but were the kinds of songs that could be
covered by every washed-up crooner who should have been made
superfluous by the advent of Elvis (in the late sixties, Elvis hadn't yet
become a washed-up crooner himself). Webb's hits of this period fall
into two basic categories: innocuous pop songs, like "Up, Up, and
Away," that could be easily turned into advertising jingles, and
melodramatic pop songs, like the Brooklyn Bridge's "Worst That Could
Happen," that far too many people misconstrued as being romantic
and showing true emotion.

In 1968 Webb wrote and produced an entire album for actor Richard
Harris, whose previous calling card was his performance as King
Arthur in the film version of *Camelot*. The album, *A Tramp Shining*,
proved to be another major hit for Webb. But long after the album has
disappeared and been forgotten, its hit single, "MacArthur Park,"
refuses to die.

For more than seven minutes Harris emotes his way through Webb's
bathetic lyrics to love lost. "Spring was never waiting for us, girl./It ran
one step ahead as we waited in the dance," Harris breathlessly sings.
What? Harris proceeds with ever slighter images of his life's one great
love until we get to that wonderfully incomprehensible chorus that
supposedly sums it all up. Let's all sing together: "MacArthur's Park is
melting in the dark/All the sweet cream icing flowing down/I don't
think that I can take it/'Cause it took so long to bake it/And I'll never
have that recipe again." If the best comparison he can make to her
leaving is a cake melting in the rain, then is it any wonder she didn't
stick around?

As over-the-top ludicrous as Harris's vocalizing is, it takes a back seat to
Webb's arrangement. From its piano and harpsichord opening, you
know deep down that this is going to be one of the most pretentious
recordings ever made. Showing off a range of musical styles that runs
from the overorchestrated to the ridiculously overorchestrated, Webb
pulls out every arrangement cliché he can remember: clashing cym-
bals, swirling strings, multiple minicrescendos, lines punctuated with
blasts of brass, and many another well-worn hook are thrown in until

the climactic heavenly choir prepares us for the big fade. The most musically interesting part of the song is the uptempo "Sixties au Go-Go" section near the end that sounds like Webb's attempt to pass classical gas more than a month before Mason Williams's successful release of the same name.

The only thing that prevented "MacArthur Park" from reaching number one was Herb Alpert's version of "This Guy's in Love With You," showing that the pop charts had slipped into one of their periodic comas. "MacArthur Park" infested the charts on two more occasions: first in 1971 when the Four Tops took it to number thirty-eight, and again in 1978 when Donna Summer topped the charts with it. One suspects a rap version is imminent.

One more version also hit the charts. Waylon Jennings went Top Forty on the country chart with "MacArthur Park" in 1969 and earned a Grammy for it. We can only assume that ol' Waylon had a strong urge to get the sickening taste of the song out of his mouth, because his next single was a cover of Chuck Berry's "Brown-Eyed Handsome Man." Apparently his fans wanted to forget the whole experience too, because they bought enough copies to push the follow-up to number three.

DON MCLEAN
"American Pie—Parts I and II"
United Artists, 1971
highest chart position: number one (four weeks)

No doubt about it, the sixties were dead. The Beatles had broken up, Motown was waning, and Brian Wilson was already beyond reclamation. If that wasn't evidence enough, the singles charts in 1971 were being dominated by Bread, the Osmonds, and the Carpenters. Sure, Al Green or the Rolling Stones would occasionally crack the Top Ten; even Neil Young had a number-one hit with "Heart of Gold," but that was a fluke, not to mention one of his lighter numbers. Usually we were stuck with the likes of "Precious and Few" by Climax.

Contributing to this void was Don McLean and "American Pie," a panoramic view of the rock landscape. The linchpin of his eight-and-a-half-minute opus is the death of Buddy Holly, which, even before McLean copped the phrase, was known as "the day the music died." McLean bemoans the death of this early rock-and-roll innovator (who went down with Ritchie Valens and the Big Bopper in an air crash on February 3, 1959), which is fine by us, but then he overstays his welcome (*way* overstays his welcome), going on to offer an unasked-for critique of music during the sixties.

Once you start listening to the words, you're left wondering: "What is this guy talking about?" Couched in terms so symbolically obscure that commentators and high-school English students had a field day trying to find their meaning, "American Pie" presented a whole cast of sixties musicians in glib caricatures (Dylan as "the Jester") or hazy metaphors. He was probably talking about the Beatles as the "Sergeants [Pepper, we presume] playing a marching tune," but who could be sure? Twenty years later, we're still not sure of some of his images. When he sang about Satan standing on the stage, was he referring to Mick Jagger? Jim Morrison? Neil Diamond? Who knows? Who cares?

There are a couple of good things to be said about "American Pie." The first is that it provoked more interest in Buddy Holly than at any time since his death. The second is that the song was so long that it had to be cut in half to fit on a single (hence, "Parts I and II"). Many Top Forty stations refused to play the whole song; often we only had to hear the first half. Finally, its incredible success annoyed McLean. He got so sick of talking about the song and playing it in concert that he refused; in turn, audiences refused him. And no one ever did figure out what he was talking about.

JIMMY GILMER AND THE FIREBALLS
"Sugar Shack"
Dot, 1963

highest chart position: number one (five weeks)

One of our favorite reissues of the early eighties was Buddy Holly's *For the First Time Anywhere*, a set that reclaimed some of the seminal rocker's most visceral early performances from the indifferent overdubs producer Norman Petty slapped on them after Holly went down in Clear Lake. Those ferocious takes (you have to hear what Holly does to "I'm Gonna Set My Foot Down") throw into relief the inadequacies of Petty's later discoveries, the Fireballs, the bozos who watered down Holly's fiery originals with their own sluggish playing. Never was a band so misnamed.

The shortcomings displayed on the Holly material become far more apparent on their own records. "Bottle of Wine," one of the Fireballs' biggest hits (it was to reach number nine, number nine, number nine), represents the kind of mid-sixties, white-boy rock and roll put out by people who never realized that there had been a British Invasion, let alone heard of Motown. In late 1967, after records like *Sgt. Pepper's Lonely Hearts Club Band* had forever changed the requirements of rock (for better and worse), the Fireballs released this third-rate frat song, the likes of which had gone out of style years before.

Sung in a voice that tries its best to sound gruff and ruff but comes off about as raunchy as the Bill Justis song of that name, "Bottle of Wine" belies its intention as a down-and-dirty anthem: its bouncy melody and sing-along lyrics are more appropriate to Cub Scouts on a hike. The guitar solo, which was buried in the mix (not quite deeply enough), sounds as though the player picked up the instrument for the first time that minute. This guy backed tapes of Buddy Holly? They had to be tapes, because Holly, despite his reputation for excessive politeness, probably wouldn't have even let him into the studio.

As bad as "Bottle of Wine" is, it ain't the band's previous assault on the Top Ten, "Sugar Shack." Jimmy Gilmer, lead singer for the Fireballs, warbles the lyrics with a syrupy voice (yeah, we know, "Saccharine Shack") that renders every syllable completely unbelievable. Gilmer's undersinging here may help to explain the pseudogrowl used on "Bottle of Wine": overcompensation five years after the fact is as good an explanation as any.

The lyrics demonstrate the time-space continuum problems that many bad songs exhibit when they try to relate a story. Gilmer spends the first two verses singing about how he's going to go back to the ol' shack to get the girl he left behind there. Then, before we even know if he's gotten there or not, he's married to her and making plans to go back to the sugar shack again! Doesn't it seem like there's a verse missing somewhere? Sure, it's only a two-and-a-half-minute pop song, but if you're going to tell us a story, let's have a beginning, a middle, and an end. What they should have done was add another verse to the end in which they go back and find out that the sugar shack has become a bar. The singer buys a "bottle of wine," dumps his wife, and begins a life of destitution. Now we're starting to have a song. But we really shouldn't expect so much from any supposed rock-and-roll song in which the lead instrument is a flute (we'll get to Jethro Tull).

"Sugar Shack" was number one for five weeks. The only good thing that can be said for it is that it pushed Bobby Vinton's "Blue Velvet" out of the top spot. (Yeah, we're David Lynch fans, but come on!) Then again, in its turn it was displaced by "Deep Purple" by Nino Tempo and April Stevens. And who says rock and roll wasn't dead before the Beatles showed up?

LINDA RONSTADT
"Back in the U.S.A."
Asylum, 1978
highest chart position: number sixteen

We've deliberated for months. The most believable explanation we can come up with is that part of Linda Ronstadt's brain, the part that has to do with discriminating between good and bad musical ideas, atrophied when she was a child. Ronstadt, a singer with remarkable technical proficiency, has set her larynx on everything: rock, country-rock, straight country, new wave, opera, prerock pop, *norteño* music, Bulgarian folk music, you name it. Two elements characterize her performances in all arenas: a range and assurance that never fail to impress and a complete inability to place intelligently those rare gifts at the service of the song. Whether she's singing a standard accompanied by the Nelson Riddle Orchestra or a Phil Spector chestnut with the help of Emmylou Harris and Dolly Parton, Ronstadt is rarely involved in a song. It frequently sounds as if she hadn't been introduced to the lyrics until she began singing. And sometimes not even then.

For every credible cover Ronstadt achieves ("When Will I Be Loved" and "You're No Good" are about the top), there are dozens that call attention to her refusal to think out the songs before she opens her mouth. She has trivialized the songs of sources as varied as Smokey Robinson and Elvis Costello, the Rolling Stones and Doris Troy, Buddy Holly and Warren Zevon, Roy Orbison and Neil Young. Her 1974–80 string of Top Ten hits was defined by Peter Asher's pristine, soulless production, matched by the mechanical, one-eye-on-the-clock accompaniment of such marginal (even for L.A.) talents like Lonely Boy Andrew Gold and future TV actor John David Souther. Ronstadt, Asher, and company never tried to eke anything new out of these covers. Each time they did the same thing: made it sound tasty, made it sound sweet, made it sound like everything else they'd ever done. They even pioneered use of a fancy electronic recording device known as the Aphex aural exciter, which was supposed to sweeten the sound.

Ronstadt's most blundering cover, a perverse achievement, was her 1978 assault and battery on Chuck Berry's magical "Back in the U.S.A." Berry's detailed fable of our nation's most modest charms has been covered by hundreds of notable performers on stage or in the studio, most notably the MC5. The vast majority of these performers were able to capture the naive exuberance that makes lines like "where hamburgers sizzle on an open grill night and day" sound like descriptions of small miracles.

Not Linda, who made this sizzler sound jaded. She has always had trouble at speedy tempos, though the fault is shared by her band members, who also have had trouble keeping up with the Eagles. Also blame producer Asher, who proved fourteen years earlier as half of Peter and Gordon that he could ruin good Lennon/McCartney songs with careless ease. This band simply can't rock, and Ronstadt delivers the words in a random, staccato manner, like she's reading a train schedule over a public-address system. At the end of the song, she tries to make her voice sound rough, but it's obvious she's showing off. Her voice says, "Hey, listen to my voice," not "Hey, listen to what I have to say." It's that thoughtless narcissism, more than anything else, that justified Ronstadt's tenure as the queen of L.A. session-rock.

ZAGER AND EVANS
"In the Year 2525 (Exordium and Terminus)"
Truth, 1968 (reissued by RCA in 1969)
highest chart position: number one (six weeks)

As William Shatner, Leonard Nimoy, and Jefferson Starship have proven, science fiction and rock and roll don't mix any better than Zsa Zsa Gabor and reality. Prime rock and roll is immediate, direct; spacey visions of the far future tend to be neither. Denny Zager and Rick Evans, in their only charting single, found a way to be as silly and vapid as an outtake from *Abbott and Costello Go to Mars*. On "In the Year 2525," Zager and Evans previewed the destruction of humanity in terms as facile and pessimistic as that of the diary-quality, doomy sci-fi read by the stoned high-school kids who kept the damn thing on top of the charts for forty days and forty nights.

Here's what to expect in Zager and Evans's melodramatic future. In 3535, our personalities will be determined by "a pill." In 4545, we'll have no teeth or eyes, which won't be a problem because, after all, "nobody's gonna look at you." Body parts continue to melt away; by 5555, we won't need limbs ("your legs got nothing to do") and sex will be passé by 6565. Perhaps the only solace we can take in our desensing is the likelihood that in this future we won't be able to hear any Zager and Evans songs.

Like most bad science fiction, "In the Year 2525" invokes a superior being to force a fake climax (so much for sex being outmoded). Having exhausted all five words they can think of that rhyme with *five*, Zager and Evans double the ante: "In the year 7510/If God's a-comin'/He oughta make it by then." According to our prophets, God ponders Judgment Day, which He doesn't get around to until 8510. (He's getting lazy in his old age. It only took Him a week to put it all together.) Devolution continues, in a tale that quickly becomes more chronologically muddled than *The Sound and the Fury*. By the time we get to the year 10000 (they don't mention if people still start the dates on their checks with a 9), ecology becomes an issue (our soothsayers are only eight millennia and change off), but then we find out that "maybe it's only yesterday." That clears that up.

Zager and Evans's pessimism became more direct, albeit far more gruesome. They followed up "In the Year 2525" with "Mr. Turkey," the story of a man who raped a bar pickup in Wichita Falls and, as penance, nailed his left wrist to the wall of his jail cell. The narrator didn't bleed to death until after the song ended, roughly the same time Denny and Rick went their separate ways.

PETER, PAUL, AND MARY
"I Dig Rock and Roll Music"
Warner Bros., 1967
highest chart position: number nine

Sometimes a useful movement needs a bland face to push it into the consciousness of mainstream America. For Bob Dylan and sixties folk music, the blandest faces and voices belonged to future pardoned felon Peter Yarrow, failed actor Noel "Paul" Stookey, and flop-Broadway-show chorus girl Mary Travers. Peter, Paul, and Mary's hit versions of "Blowin' in the Wind" and "Don't Think Twice, It's All Right" gave Bob Dylan his first pop-radio exposure. These tributes are characterized primarily by an adroitness at making the composer's most potent ideas sound dull. As with more common fare like "Puff the Magic Dragon," Peter, Paul, and Mary turned the Dylan tunes into campfire sing-alongs. If there was anything provocative or probing about "Blowin' in the Wind" or "Don't Think Twice, It's All Right," you'd never know it from these homogenized versions.

Peter, Paul, and Mary always sounded smug (you can almost hear them say, "We're so much cooler than you are for knowing about Dylan before you did. Nyah"), and they quickly turned petulant after Dylan started scoring his own hits. By the Summer of Love, Peter, Paul, and Mary were mad as hell—their most recent single, 1966's "The Other Side of This Life," had spent only a week on the charts (at number one hundred) before disappearing—and they weren't going to take it anymore. They thought, how dare these upstarts dislodge us from the charts? We're...we're...we're...artists! We'll show them what we think of them!

Hence "I Dig Rock and Roll Music," the most condescending song ever written about the form. Peter, Paul, and Mary show their hand immediately: Stookey sings the first line, the title of the song, trying to sound rough, like a bona fide rock singer. Instead he sounds fake, like a middle-aged Vegas crooner desperately trying to reel in the kids by covering a contemporary pop hit. If you're going to make fun of rock and roll in a rock-and-roll song (which can be done: listen to the Byrds' "So You Want to Be a Rock 'n' Roll Star," or even Pink Floyd's "Have a Cigar"), you can't sound this stiff. Stookey is trying to be subversive— railing at the rock industry within the confines of the form—but you can't be subversive if you're not persuasive.

Throughout "I Dig Rock and Roll Music," Peter, Paul, and Mary betray their ignorance of rock and roll. They are so out of touch that their examples of performers to make fun of are the Mamas and the Papas (who "nail us to the wall" when "the words don't get in the way") and Donovan (whose quiet, nasal singing is belittled). Peter, Paul, and Mary are picking on easy, false targets: anyone around in the summer of *Sgt. Pepper* knew that the Mamas, the Papas, and Donovan weren't what was happening. The occasional psychedelic touches—indifferent backward tapes and all that, not to mention the word *groovy*—hint at the zeitgeist, but they are so clumsy they're just distractions.

As you'd expect, these dour finger-pointers can't let the record end without a moral. Furious that they can't write trite homilies that two-year-olds will understand and have the country love them, Peter, Paul, and Mary declaim, "I think I could really say something/If you know what I mean/But if I really say it/The radio won't play it/Unless I lay it between the lines." Of course, folks: that's why you didn't title this record "I Hate the Guts of People Who Make More Money than Us Playing Rock-and-Roll Music." This record is about a trio who can sense that they're on the way out refusing to acknowledge that the rules of the pop game have changed. Like prerock performers pushed out of the way by Elvis, Peter, Paul, and Mary longed for a time before these kids started crowding out "good music." By 1967, they sounded like parents.

CHARLENE
"I've Never Been to Me"
Motown, 1982 (reissue of 1977 independent single)
highest chart position: number three

CHARLENE AND STEVIE WONDER
"Used to Be"
Motown, 1982
highest chart position: number forty-six

Some rock stars spend their careers singing about the endless pleasures of the rock life. The biggest problem with such boasting, as everyone from Ted Nugent to R.E.O. Speedwagon has found out, is that you eventually alienate your audience. After all, it's safe to say that most people buying a record don't play to sold-out sports arenas on a regular basis. People want their rock stars to speak to their lives.

Many people also want to hear that the life of a rock star isn't so great after all, and that's where mush like "I've Never Been to Me" by Charlene (full name: Charlene Duncan) fits in. Her only solo single that snuck past number ninety-six, this Muzak-ready ballad is extremely cynical in its pandering to an unglamorous audience. I'll tell you how lucky you are not to be stars, the song says, and then maybe you'll buy enough records so Charlene can keep living the life of a star. Of course you'll still be in the doldrums.

After a piano intro that could have been sampled off a Chicago outtake, Charlene accosts some poor, innocent woman on the street. "Hey, lady/You, lady," she purrs like one of those Dianetics robots on the street corner who want you to take a personality test (if you have any personality, you fail the test). She goes on sadly about how glamorous her life has been, but notes, "I wish someone had talked to me like I wanna talk to you." As late as the second verse, she's still trying to convince her victim to stick around: "Please, lady/Please, lady/Don't just walk away." We can't see if Charlene has resorted to handcuffs.

For whatever reason (boredom? fear? pity?), the woman keeps listening to Charlene's made-up tale of woe. Surprisingly, she doesn't Mace Charlene when the singer whines at her, "I've been undressed by kings/And seen some things/That a woman ain't supposed to see." Like what? The secret man handshake?

Assuming Charlene now has her heel embedded in the woman's neck, she proceeds with a spoken section in which the would-be Bhagwan expresses her philosophy in words that would befuddle both L. Ron Hubbard and Lyndon LaRouche. In a serious voice usually employed only by Peter, Paul, and Mary in National Public Radio interviews, Charlene says, "Hey, you know what paradise is? It's a lie, a fantasy we create about people and places as we'd like them to be. But you know what truth is? It's that little baby you're holding. And it's the man you fought with this morning—the same one you're gonna make love with tonight. That's truth. That's love."

By now we're sure the woman is gagging, but the orchestra has swelled up so loudly we can't hear her reaction to Charlene's plaint that "Sometimes I get to crying/For unborn children/That might have made me complete." No doubt the woman broke free and ran screaming. Listen, Charlene: if you want to have a normal family life, if you no longer want to "move like Harlow/In Monte Carlo," get a real job. Otherwise, stop complaining.

Charlene got her break at Motown because she was one of Stevie Wonder's protégés. Sensing that his find couldn't carry another song on her own, Stevie moved in to shore up his investment and recorded a duet with her, "Used to Be," which used the same hack songwriters as its predecessor and was even more emotionally manipulative: there's a crucifixion scene in the clincher verse.

You know you're in trouble when a song starts with the disemboweled logic of "Superman was killed in Dallas/There's no love left in the palace/Someone took the Beatles' lead guitar." Christopher Reeve is alive and well (and George Reeves died elsewhere), George Harrison's Gretsch is safe and sound, and we'll assume that some royalty are as capable of love as we serfs. Charlene sings so sweetly you're afraid she raided your pantry, and Stevie's puffy delivery makes his vocal on "I Just Called to Say I Love You" seem tough. More nostalgic anachronisms appear and immediately evaporate, such as, "Used to be a knight in shining armor/Didn't have to own a shiny car." Listen, dopes, if Lancelot had had access to a Benz, he would have bought one. The song finally disintegrates into Stevie asking "Does your president have soul?" and complaining in the most unoriginal terms that all these ungrateful, unloved kids nowadays do nothing but cut school and smoke grass. Fortunately, this was not a big hit. If it had been, its narcotizing effect would have left the Medellín cartel envious. All we can say to "Used to Be" is just say no. Most people did. Charlene hasn't had a charting pop single since. We hope she's living a nice, normal life.

THINK
"Once You Understand"
Laurie, 1971
highest chart position: number twenty-three

Before the gender gap, we had the gener-
ation gap. Strange thing, that generation gap. Although most of it was
the fault of those older folks set in their ways (a nation of Spiro
Agnews), those on the younger side also seemed to be quite capable of
acting with intolerant idiocy. Would you want Paul Kantner arguing for
your side? Such young guns were the people championed by producers
Lou Stallman and Bobby Susser and their studio-misnomered Think.

"Once You Understand" immediately slumps into neutral with an *a
cappella* chant of "Things get a little easier/Once you understand." It's
more than a little sappy—the uncredited male singer sounds like one of
those "I'd Like to Teach the World to Sing" vocalists—but the country
was being torn apart by so much ugliness in 1971 that you were willing
to give any plea for empathy the benefit of the doubt, at least until the
end of the first verse.

Unfortunately, the first verse never appears. The two-line chant gets
picked up by a dozen other singers who'd like to stop doing jingles for a
living, and, along with a mild drum rhythm, that chant becomes the
backing track for a series of brief dialogues. That's right, "Once You
Understand" is early performance art, a series of vignettes that are
supposed to show how distant the generations in America have
become. Deep, man.

The first sound comes from a middle-aged father character. "I'll be
expecting you to get a haircut by Friday," he says.

"Forget it, Dad," comes the self-righteous teenage retort. "It won't
change anything."

"Forget nothing," Dad shoots back. "You'll do as I say as long as you're
living in my house."

It's Mom's turn to act insensitive toward her son. "He knows I'm not
feeling well," she says, as if she has just swallowed a set of mah-jongg
tiles, "and yet he doesn't take one second out to help his mother. His
only concern is for himself."

"Come on, Ma!" the boy snivels back. "Whaddya want from me?"

"Don't argue with your mother!" interrupts fascist father figure. "Just
shut up and listen!"

It's chorus time again; the wrestlers all go back to their corners, tag their replacements, and—Ding!—round two.

"But Mom," whines a teenage girl, "all my friends will be there."

"I said no," says a staccato mom. "You can't go."

"But why?" the daughter asks, already deciding which window is the best for sneaking out after her mom dozes off in front of the RCA during "The Courtship of Eddie's Father."

"I don't want you in that neighborhood."

"Why?" sniffles little Ms. Know-It-All. "What's wrong with that neighborhood?"

"I don't like the kind of people living there."

"What's wrong with them?" This is not what Socrates envisioned. And besides, we want to know who *they* are.

"Never mind," Mom says. "Someday you'll thank me."

During the next chorus, the many repetitions of "Things get a little easier/Once you understand" lead the jingle warblers actually to believe what they're singing, and the percussion backing makes the whole thing sound like a day on the Common with another brainwashed group, the Hari Krishnas.

Meanwhile, back in Uptightland...

Mom has awoken from her nap, suddenly thrust into consciousness by a dream in which she married Bill Bixby and together they raised her children right. "Are you sure nobody kept you company tonight while you were babysitting?"

"What's that supposed to mean?" the daughter asks.

"Just curious," Mom says, all sarcasm.

This of course makes the kid self-righteous. "Admit it, Mom," she says. "You don't trust me."

We're more than halfway into the song. It sounds like the United Nations should call in Henry Kissinger and Le Duc Tho, but producers

Stallman and Susser aren't interested in rapprochement. All they want are more easy examples of dumb parents. On to the next scene.

"Where are you going now?" By now, Mom is a real wreck.

"To my friend's house," says the son, who still hasn't cut his hair.

"Don't you have things to do in the house?" she asks. "Don't you have any homework?" she asks, before he can answer the first question. "Why don't you sit down and read a book?"

The son has his response down. "Oh, Ma."

"Don't 'Oh, Ma' me," Mom barks. "You're wasting your life away with foolish things."

Smug son: "What are you talking about? How about the bridge club and your ladies' groups and the parties and your daytime programs? What about all that?"

"That's different." Not a good answer, but an answer worthy of "Oh, Ma."

Here comes the daughter who pets during babysitting, probably with one of *those* people. "Ma, I'll be home at eleven."

"You'd better be home at ten," Mom says as she collapses on the plastic-covered couch. "Or don't bother to come home at all." We can picture her changing the locks at 10:01.

Back to the failed male-bonding with which we began "Once You Understand." The father says, "When I was your age, I was working twelve hours a day, six days a week, to help pay for the food and the rent."

"I don't understand," the boy sasses back, unable to see beyond the hair in front of his face. "What's that got to do with me?"

"If you can't figure that out for yourself," the father says, "you're stupid."

The kid, suddenly wonderful, tries a new tack. "Hey, Dad, did you see my new guitar? I joined a group."

"Son, there's little bit more to life than joining a group and playing guitar."

The kid can hardly hear him. "Yeah, Dad," he says back mindlessly. "What is there to life?" The word *life* echoes behind them, because the producers think it means something. What it means, they're not sure, but definitely something. "Life...life...life...life."

As sudden as a stroke, the backup singers and tired drummer disappear. After a moment of silence that's no doubt intended to be a substitute for drama, we hear a new voice. It's authoritative. It's even-tempered. It must be the fuzz.

"Mr. Cook?"

"Yes?" Dad sounds confused.

"Do you have a son named Robert, Robert Cook, age seventeen?"

"Yes."

"I'm sorry, Mr. Cook," the cop intones. "You'd better come down to the station house." He pauses for a moment, and then adds. "Your son is dead."

The father is immediately devastated. "Dead? H-how?"

"He died of an overdose."

"M-my God," the father says and breaks down. He's learned the stupid moral of "Once You Understand": if you don't approve of everything your teenaged child does, he will kill himself just to spite you. (On the other hand, maybe if the parents were more strict, their son never would have gone into *that* neighborhood to buy smack.)

But all is not lost for those of us still on this plane. While the actor playing Dad pretends to cry, the angelic voice that opened the track returns. "Things get a little easier/Once you understand," he sings. There's echo in his voice to indicate that he's in heaven. He died for our sins and he wants us to make it better. So folks, tell your kids you love them. And kids, let your parents know that deep down you couldn't do anything without them. But leave us out of it. We're trying to figure out why the dead kid's body is at the station house.

Have you hugged your kid today?

CHUCK BERRY
"My Ding-a-Ling"
Chess, 1972
highest chart position: number one (two weeks)

Chuck Berry has been served with many injustices in his time: Abuse at the hands of concert promoters, prison terms for offenses no white man would see jail for, cover versions of his songs by the Beach Boys, etc. One of the greatest, however, is that none of his wry fifties and sixties singles for Chess, among the most essential in all rock and roll, ever became a number-one hit. We live in a world that allows "You Light Up My Life" to clutter the top of the charts for ten weeks but leaves no room for "Johnny B. Goode," "Roll Over Beethoven," or "Memphis" to hit it for even one. It's enough to make you pop your eardrums.

You might want to push that sharp pin in a little deeper when you discover that "My Ding-a-Ling" was Berry's sole chart-topper. Recording live at the Lancaster Arts Festival in Coventry, England, Berry introduces "My Ding-a-Ling" as "our alma mater" and as a "fourth-grade ditty" in his interminable introduction (the LP version of "My Ding-a-Ling," on *The London Chuck Berry Sessions*, rambled on for 11:33), but in fact the song is far less mature. "We have one more left to do," Berry says just before the song, and the crowd voices its disapproval. It's as if they know what's coming.

"My Ding-a-Ling" strings together double-entendre penis jokes that can be enjoyed only by the very young or the very drunk. There were enough of both at Coventry that night to join in for a lengthy sing-along, although that didn't stop Chuck from exhorting more to join in: "Those of you who will not sing," he rasps hoarsely, "you must be playing with your own ding-a-ling." So there Berry was, arguably the most direct songwriter in all rock and roll, reduced to begging drunk Brit kids to sing about masturbation. "That's future Parliament out there singing," Berry warns at one point (by now you get the idea that he doesn't get around to much singing here), implying that not singing along is a bad career move for the crowd.

Back on these shores, we were so confused (Nixon was on his way to a landslide) that we placed "My Ding-a-Ling" at the top of the pop chart. Berry's first audience, the rhythm-and-blues crowd, was much wiser. This bathroom-joke exercise from the former rhythmic master was so unfunky that it didn't reach higher than number forty-two on the R&B chart. Berry should have taken the hint: after this album, he never had another hit. However, there is now a generation of young adults who think that Chuck Berry was just the guy who did "My Ding-a-Ling." Bye-bye, Johnny.

Special Sections

The Brian Jones Memorial List

Sometimes a change of key personnel can reinvigorate a group (we're thinking of the Drifters, the Dominoes, and most of all the Soul Stirrers). Most of the time, however, a key individual *is* a band's identity and the remaining members have no business trudging on without him. Here are some of the most glaring examples of personnel changes that flopped.

Van Halen. What made this heavy-metal colossus intermittently interesting was the tension between show-biz singer David Lee Roth and excessive guitarist Eddie Van Halen. Once Sammy Hagar took Roth's place, all that was left was the excess and, ta da!, no point.

Lynyrd Skynyrd. Beware tribute tours, especially when they're led by a relative of one of the deceased.

Starship. When Jefferson Airplane/Starship founding members Paul Kantner and Grace Slick left the band, we hoped they'd start a band called the Jeffersons. No such luck.

The Blue Ridge Rangers. Face it: after John Fogerty left, they were never the same.

Emerson, Lake, and Palmer. Granted, they were always useless. But when Keith Emerson and Greg Lake temporarily checked their egos at the door and decided to re-form in 1986 without drummer Carl Palmer, they called in Cozy Powell to replace him so that they could keep the ELP trademark.

The Doors. Ray Manzarek couldn't play organ without sounding full of himself. Imagine how he sang. He later put out a solo record, *The Whole Thing Started with Rock and Roll, Now It's Out of Control* (Mercury, 1975).

J. Geils Band. Peter Wolf's defection from the band at the height of its popularity ruined everyone's career. The one album the remaining members attempted was full of breast jokes, hooks we recognized from *Freeze-Frame*, and keyboardist Seth Justman uncomfortable and sagging in his new role as singer.

The Red Bank Rockers. E Street saxophonist Clarence Clemons made an extraordinary find in soul vocalist J. T. Bowen. By the group's second record, Bowen was gone and Clarence was mugging with Jackson Browne and his incompetent actress-actress girlfriend. Big Man, what happened?

Genesis. Sure they sell more records now. But would you rather listen to Phil Collins or Peter Gabriel?

Fleetwood Mac. This group is legendary for its ability to turn over members yet still make fine music. But the loss of lead guitarist/weirdo Lindsey Buckingham was the figurative end of the road. Replacement guitarists Rick Vito and Billy Burnette are natural sidemen with second-tier ideas; they have no business writing and singing songs with a band this musically savvy.

The Who. Keith Moon may not have been the Who's guiding force, but he was the most important element of this great band's chemistry. On their 1989 tour, the surviving trio added twelve members to compensate for the loss of the Moon. They didn't come close.

The Clash. After Joe Strummer fired Mick Jones (for political reasons, they said at the time, although Strummer soon blamed the sacking on manager Bernie Rhodes and unsuccessfully begged Jones to return), he hired some kid off the street (we could look it up, but his name is unimportant) because he looked and sounded a bit like Jones. Needless to say, this conglomeration lasted only one album.

Grateful Dead. Unsteady from the start, they lost what little grounding they had when keyboardist Ron "Pigpen" McKernan drank himself to death and the Godchauxes hopped on board. The pair turned out to be so bad that even the other members of

the band realized they had to go. Perhaps the rock world would be best served if everyone left.

Mott the Hoople. Some purists felt that these glam-rock mavens should have packed it in after Mick Ralphs quit to form Bad Company, but at least they still had songwriter and singer Ian Hunter (who brought in guitarist Mick Ronson). When Hunter and Ronson left, however, there really was no reason to continue, but nobody bothered to tell the rest of the group until after they put out two more albums.

Sam and Dave. Even before Dave Prater died, Sam Moore was touring with many other lesser singers, few of whom were called Dave by their mothers. One of them was indiscriminate script approver Dan Aykroyd.

The Velvet Underground. Without Lou Reed?

The Band. At the Last Waltz in 1976, mouthpiece Robbie Robertson promised that the group's touring days were over. The four other Band members must not have been listening, because they toured incessantly through the eighties and into the nineties without Robertson, even after the death of pianist Richard Manuel.

Special Notice

The Blue Notes (without Teddy Pendergrass, not Harold Melvin)

The Commodores (without Lionel Ritchie)

The Drifting Cowboys (without Hank Williams)

The Furious Five (without Grandmaster Flash)

The Jacksons (without Michael)

The Miracles (without Smokey Robinson)

The Rock 'n' Roll Trio (without Johnny Burnette)

The Rumour (without Graham Parker)

The Supremes (without Diana Ross)

Badfinger (still touring although two members have committed suicide)

We recognize those performers who are obviously less talented than their better-known siblings but still won't shut up.

Dave Davies (lead guitarist for the Kinks). Dave founded the Kinks, then invited his brother Ray to join. Turns out that Ray is a rock-and-roll song-writing genius; turns out that Dave can't write a song outside the confines of the group to save his recording contract. Literally. Dave has released three solo albums on three different labels. None made any effort to pick up his option.

Chris Jagger (brother of Mick and solo artist of no renown). On the positive side, his lips are much smaller than Mick's; on the negative side, so is his talent.

Simon Townshend (brother of Pete and solo artist of even less renown than Chris). Come to think of it, this isn't a phenomenon monopolized by rock stars. Anybody remember baseball's Tommy Aaron?

Mike McGear. Never heard of him? That's because he changed his name so people wouldn't think he was cashing in on brother Paul McCartney's success. Then again, maybe he changed it after hearing Paul's work on Wings' *Wild Life.*

Johnny Van Zant. As late as 1990, he was still regularly writing songs about hangin' out with his brother Ronnie Van Zant, the heart of Lynyrd Skynyrd who died thirteen years earlier. Wake up!

LaToya Jackson (failed sister of Michael). Janet bared her soul on *Control* and sold five million records; LaToya bared everything else and was treated like the joke she was.

Let's recognize those who tried to turn a quick profit by cashing in on an association (however fleeting) with a popular performer, especially the most popular: the Beatles.

Pete Best. The Beatles drummer was fired from the band (with good reason) just prior to the group's first recording session for EMI. Best later released an album titled *Best of the Beatles* (a clever—not to mention cleverly misleading—title).

Louise Harrison Caldwell. George Harrison's sister; at the height of Beatlemania, she released an album titled *All about the Beatles*.

The GTOs. What does one call the GTOs? To define them as a band is to give them more musical credit than they would ever deserve. They're more like a blare of strumpets. The GTOs were a collection of Los Angeles–based groupies who, under the twisted direction (in more ways than one) of Frank Zappa, released two albums for his custom label in the late 1960s. That label wasn't called Bizarre for nothing.

Tony Sheridan. Another Beatles cash-in. Sheridan was *the* rock star in Hamburg, Germany, when the Beatles were playing strip clubs along the Reeperbahn, the German version of Times Square (with even less charm). The Beatles backed Sheridan for just one failed recording session. Sheridan's manager must have been standing in line right behind Pete Best at the cash-in counter, because these tracks were suddenly released all over the world when the Beatles shot to the top.

Elvis's family. This group includes hairdressers, members of the Memphis Mafia, and especially the aunt who wrote the *Elvis Presley Cook Book*. Pass the fried peanut butter.

Special Bob Dylan Section

The Ten Worst Dylanesque Songwriting Ripoffs

1. "Eve of Destruction," **BARRY McGUIRE**

2. "Dawn of Correction," **THE SPOKESMEN**

3. "A Simple Desultory Phillipic (or How I Was Robert McNamara'd into Submission)," **SIMON AND GARFUNKEL**

4. "Understand Your Man," **JOHNNY CASH**

5. "The Sound of Silence," **SIMON AND GARFUNKEL**

6. "Mary Queen of Arkansas," **BRUCE SPRINGSTEEN**

7. "Lincoln Limousine," **JERRY LEE LEWIS**

8. "American Roulette," **ROBBIE ROBERTSON**

9. "We Didn't Start the Fire," **BILLY JOEL**

10. "American Pie," **DON McLEAN**

The Worst Cover
Versions of Bob Dylan Songs

As the greatest rock-and-roll song-writer who isn't Chuck Berry or Smokey Robinson, Bob Dylan has a catalogue that remains unrivaled. Unfortunately, it hasn't remained un-pillaged. Since Dylan at his peak was the very definition of popular hipness, many useless performers (or worthy ones temporarily disconnected from their muse) reasoned that they could perform a Dylan song and get instant credibility! Instant hit! What follows are some of the most wrongheaded attempts to marry a Bob Dylan song to a totally incompatible performance style.

William Shatner, **"Mr. Tambourine Man"** *(Decca, 1986)*. This song makes one wonder if perhaps Captain Kirk dropped too much acid during his five-year mission. All of his album *A Transformed Man* is overdramatic mush (check out "Lucy in the Sky with Diamonds" and the Shakespeare solil-oquies), but "Mr. Tambourine Man"'s orbit of lunacy is by far the LP's wildest. In a tack we'll soon see again, Shatner decides that the best way to pull out the tune's every passion is to recite it like poetry. Shatner, whose overwrought performances as T. J. Hooker and the unctuous host of "Rescue 911" have never been mistaken for competent acting, missteps even more horribly when we can't see what we're laughing at. After a woodwind intro that might make sense in a Warner Brothers cartoon, Shatner's "Mr. Tambourine Man" starts off as bad hipster jazz, accompanied by—how symbolic!—an overamplified tambourine played on the off beat, until the music begins to resemble the beginning of the theme to "The Jetsons." Mistaking the lyrics for King Lear's speech in the middle of the storm, Shatner turns into a lysergic version of Richard Burton at his most melodramatic. He invests each line with either significantly more or less emotion than is called for, and he occasionally puts emphasis on the wrong word in the sentence or pauses at the wrong spot to make clear that he has no idea what he is doing. Smooth backup singers moan the chorus at odd intervals—or at least push him to finish the damn thing. But our Captain will accept no subordination. He screams louder and louder after the song is supposed to end, like a kid running after an ice-cream truck, finally screeching the song's title *a cappella* after the studio musicians have wisely packed up their instruments and left for the next session, perhaps on...

Sebastian Cabot, actor. Bob Dylan, poet. a dramatic reading with music *(MGM, 1967).* In the late sixties, after his stunning performance in *The Time Machine,* Cabot was popular as Mr. French on the highly rated CBS situation comedy "Family Affair." He must have had some vendetta against the network's parent company, for on this record he disembowels eleven songs by CBS recording artist Dylan. In the first season of "Family Affair," Cabot mysteriously took ill and was replaced for nine episodes. It is widely believed that he took that time to convalesce, but we have reason to believe that he spent that time discovering the music of Bob Dylan and was so moved by the find that he felt compelled to bring Dylan's songs and ideas to a new audience, namely middle-aged dimwits who might buy a Dylan record only by accident—or if Cabot's legendary thespian name was associated with it. On *Sebastian Cabot, actor. Bob Dylan, poet. a dramatic reading with music.* Cabot does for Bob Dylan what Mr. French did for the Davis home: cleaned it up until nothing was where it should be and everyone was confused. It you don't care about the music and want to hear Dylan's songs recited, this is for you.

Edie Brickell and the New Bohemians, **"A Hard Rain's a-Gonna Fall"** *(MCA, 1989).* Although Brickell and her Grateful Dead wanna-be accompanists had only recorded one album before they released this cover as part of the *Born on the Fourth of July* soundtrack, we already had the kind of deep aversion to her that usually takes years to accumulate. (Have we mentioned Joni Mitchell?) Brickell's spacey Rickie Lee Jones imitations, coupled with her unearned massive success and inability to stand still, made her hits like the Popeye-derived "What I Am" and "Little Miss S" such annoyances. Here Brickell turned her dubious gifts to a real song and showed how empty her method really was. The longer she holds syllables, the less they mean.

Rod Stewart, **"Forever Young"** *(Warner Bros., 1988).* This is not the place to lament the massive mid-seventies sellout that changed Rod Stewart from one of rock and roll's purest, most energetic acts into one of its most complacent and predictable, but a quick listen to Stewart's changing approach to Dylan songs (his early-seventies covers of "Tomorrow Is a Long Time" and "Only a Hobo" are definitive) tells much of the story. This is as much a rip-off as a cover. Although this "Forever Young" is credited to Stewart and two of the nobodies in his band, it has the same chord structure, melody line, title, and words as Dylan's original. Stewart's violation of the copyright laws aside, this synth-heavy ballad is pushy and melodramatic where his earlier Dylan covers were persuasive and sly.

Heaven, **"Knockin' on Heaven's Door"** *(Columbia, 1986)* and Guns N' Roses, **"Knockin' on Heaven's Door"** *(Geffen, 1990).* Dylan as heavy-metal balladeer? We'll pass, thanks.

Olivia Newton-John, **"If Not for You"** *(Uni, 1971).* Malaria Neutron-Bomb destroys a minor Dylan ditty here, but what makes this cover version, complete with annoying slide-guitar repetitions, especially repellent is that it launched the career of the soft, bland non-emoter.

The Worst Cover Versions by Bob Dylan

"Big Yellow Taxi" (from *Dylan*). Why on earth did Bob Dylan even consider covering this song? It came from the same sessions that saw the former Great White Wonder doing material by Paul Simon and Gordon Lightfoot, giving the sense that the theme was "Dylan Does the New Dylans." Since dense Canadian folk-rock-jazz-whatever dilettante Joni Mitchell was the first of the female New Dylans, we can only guess that Bob decided to give her equal time; unfortunately, he chose the wrong song. Mitchell's whiny, confessional ballads had yielded fine cover versions before, most notably Tom Rush's rendition of "Urge for Going," and we'll even give credit to Judy Collins for her take on "Both Sides Now," but any way you look at it, a song based on the notion that "they paved paradise/And put up a parking lot" is not going to be worth hearing.

Kris Kristofferson's **"They Killed Him"** (from *Knocked Out Loaded*). This song about the deaths of various messianic figures makes Dion's "Abraham, Martin, and John" seem hardheaded. Besides, you know a song is in trouble when the producer tries to save it with a children's chorus. Dylan with a children's chorus?

Curtis Mayfield's **"People Get Ready"** (from the film *Renaldo and Clara*). Dylan veers so far away from the melody, you wonder if he's singing a different song.

"Can't Help Falling in Love with You" (from *Dylan*). Dylan's version of the Elvis Presley standard features a harmonica break that sounds as if it were spliced in from another song, and a wheezy melody line that bears no relation to either Presley's original or anything that's normally considered acceptable in pop music. Dylan's singing here is as close as anyone has ever gotten to discovering the Lost Chord.

**Twenty Ideas That
Dylan Should Have
Thrown into the Garbage**

1. *Self-Portrait*
2. Christianity
3. Judaism
4. Joan Baez
5. The Grateful Dead
6. *Tarantula*
7. "Tight Connection to My Heart" video
8. *Renaldo and Clara*
9. tarot cards
10. talking to reporters (1968 to present)
11. live albums (1975 to present)
12. Jacques Levy
13. Pete Hamill's liner notes to
    Blood on the Tracks
14. Steve Douglas
15. Scarlet Rivera
16. Dave Stewart
17. acting
18. Ramblin' Jack Elliott
19. Allen Ginsberg and Lawrence Ferlinghetti
20. female backup singers

Hot Damn Tamale:
Our Special Tribute to Elvis

As if the torrent of subpar Elvis Presley packages that followed the King's death wasn't enough, we were also deluged by a flood of "tribute" records. A few were worthy of the legend (Phil Lynott's "King's Call," X's "Back 2 the Base"), but most were either quickie cash-ins, maudlin farewells, or both. Here are a few of the most ridiculous.

Daddy Bob

"Welcome Home Elvis" b/w "Papa's Gone"

Bertram International, 1977

With an angelic-echo introduction and a quick cut to the riff from "Don't Be Cruel," "Welcome Home Elvis" is the exemplar of an Elvis tribute tune. It heralds Presley's arrival in the afterlife ("all the angels have been waiting for their rock-and-roll star") and obeys the Prime Directive of Elvis tributes: if you can't think of a lyric, string together the titles of Elvis songs and hope for the best.

Jenny Nicolas

"Elvis" b/w "Daddy's Gone Bye Bye"

Philips (Denmark), 1977

Nicholas repeatedly asks, "Where are you, Elvis?" as if instead of dying, the King is playing hide-and-seek. She asks, "Where is the past that I embrace?"; she tells Elvis, "You were my cause, a different life for me," and later begs, "Elvis, please hear me calling." She doesn't get an answer by the end of the song, although she does sneak in half a dozen song titles.

George Owens

"The Gage" b/w "My Bad Dream"

World Memorial Fan Club, 1977

The sub–Scotty Moore kickoff riff of "The Gate" raises expectations, but the first lyric line—"Hi there, I'm the gate"—returns us to Tribute Hell. Here Owens imagines himself as the gate around Graceland, mourning the passing of "my boss, who was the living legend of rock and roll." At song's end, he warns that "I'm gonna close down and take it easy for a little while." We're wondering how he could possibly take it any easier than he did while he was recording this.

Brenda Joyce

"To Elvis with Love"

Tree House, 1979

Ta-da! An Elvis tribute with a particularly unctuous Las Vegas feel! These lyrics are charmingly wretched: Joyce rhymes *king* and *sing* early on, and that's only the beginning. She warbles that "He's the greatest guy we'll ever know/The great Elvis Presley, the king of [we'll let you guess]," and "Oh lord, how we miss him. He was like our own kin." Historical revisionism, another hallmark of tribute discs, also rears its head: "Nothing he recorded was ever a flop." It imagines a heavenly reunion with Gladys and God in which Elvis sings "to the only King who's greater than you are." For those keeping track, this one mentions "Teddy Bear" and "Return to Sender," among others.

George Pickard
"Elvis, the Man from Tupelo"
Bar-Tone, 1977

More revisionist history, although we wonder what Pickard meant by "Soon Sun label took him over." Like "To Elvis with Love," this song suggests an audience with God, this time involving a solid-gold guitar. Listening to these tribute records, we're flabbergasted by the widespread notion that God must have been starving for entertainment and so called Elvis home. This one lists "Blue Moon of Kentucky," "Loving You," and a dozen more.

Wilgus J.C. Rayner
"My Heart's Content (Goodbye from the King)"
RTF, 1977

The overdramatic melody of "I Was the One" is the starting point for this one, sung from Elvis's point of view, in heaven with Gladys. Here's what Elvis wants to say: "Mama, I'm with you"; "My heart's content/Jesus loves me"; "My heart's content/He asked me to sing." Rayner then goes on to describe heaven; it sounds like the angels are the new Memphis Mafia.

Tink Grimmett
"A Tribute to Elvis"
b/w "Don't Leave Me Now"
Tink, 1977

This one is as imaginative as the name of Grimmett's record label. Here we learn that "you were loved and respected by people [long pause]/ everywhere" and that "you're gone from us for now." Thanks for clearing that up, Tink. Grimmett loses ten points for not including any song titles in his lyrics.

Barry Tiffen
"Candy Bars for Elvis"
Tiffen International, 1977

Once, before he became a recording "star," Tiffen was down on his luck. Homeless in Nashville, he ducked out of a rainstorm into RCA's Studio B. Guess who was recording there that night. Guess who sent Tiff out for a candy bar. Guess who tipped him twenty dollars and said, "Here, I want you to have this." Tiffen informs us that being mistaken for a gofer "will be a part of my life forever" and "that twenty dollars, I guess, in a big way saved my life." As he's overcome with emotion, his voice breaks down toward the end of the song. Logical flaw: in the first verse Tiffen says he was stuck in Nashville because he had no car, and in a later verse we hear that he was living in a car. Either way, how come he didn't pump Elvis for a Cadillac?

Eldorado
"Just for You Dad'"
Thor, 1979

Elvis hangs out in heaven. All he does is wait for his father Vernon to die and join him in a fried-peanut-butter sandwich fiesta.

Don Todd
"I Dreamed Elvis Sang My Song"
Dale, 1977

Todd, then an aspiring songwriter (he never had a charting single), uses Presley's death as an excuse to hype one of his own songs. He sings about Elvis, and then sings some of the song he wishes Elvis had performed. Basically Todd mourns Elvis's calling because now Presley is sitting on "heaven's throne" and Todd won't get songwriting royalties.

Joy Ford
"Only Six Feet Away"
(no recording information available)

Joy dreamed for years she'd be this close to Elvis, but she wanted to be next to him, not on his grave, where her "tears fall like dew." Her abysmal singing recalls fond memories of the final scene in *Carrie*.

Billy Joel
"Elvis Presley Boulevard"
Columbia, 1982

The flip side of "Allentown" is an excuse for the hack to make fun of Elvis fans, make obvious comments about fame, and get some more mileage out of the piano riff from "Movin' Out (Anthony's Song)."

Red Sovine
"The King's Last Concert"
Gusto-Starday, 1978

This B-side of "Lay Down Sally" is a tale of a long-distance trucker so hopped up on speed he imagines he's at a posthumous Elvis show. (Elvis "had a contented gleam in his eyes." Picture that.) According to Red, "Elvis sang every song he'd done," before angels showed up, harmonized with him, and took him away. Sovine's narrator still brought in his truck late. If anything, "The King's Last Concert" is a strong argument for keeping your eyes on the road and ignoring all else. In 1980, Sovine had a fatal heart attack while driving. One wonders what he saw in his last seconds.

The Wild Honey Singers
A Child's Introduction to Elvis Presley
Kid Stuff, 1978

Presley's influence in pop has sometimes been less than welcome (heard Tom Jones lately?), but we simply cannot leave this category without shining light on one of the weirdest artifacts the King's career has inspired. The idea behind this ridiculous collection is that kids should learn to sing Elvis's songs (no argument here, although we stop short of advocating mandatory classes in early grades). But the Wild Honey Singers unintentionally turn a children's record into a comedy recording in their lengthy (both "Love Me Tender" and "Don't Be Cruel" clock in at more than seven minutes), pseudohip introductions to the songs, for which they provide sing-along aids by a Dutch Elvis impersonator who calls himself Freddy Führtenagaygen (we're guessing at the spelling). Accompanied by guitar, drums, a narrator, and a female singer (Freddy's sister, Freida) who seems to be learning the songs along with the kids, Führtenagaygen deconstructs six early Presley hits with a sneer as false as his goodwill. R.I.P., Elvis. (Kid Stuff also offers similar records for John Denver, Elton John, the Beatles, and disco.)

Camden

In the seventies, Colonel Tom Parker exploited the budget Camden reissue label for records so awful that even the main label, RCA, wouldn't consider emitting them. Pickwick bought the Camden catalogue in 1975 to give us more pointless reissues. Here are the worst:

Burning Love and Hits from His Movies, Vol. 2 (1972). A useless housecleaning, this takes a wonderful single, the title track, and pads out the record with nine songs from films like *Kissin' Cousins, Fun in Acapulco,* and *Blue Hawaii,* including one number in Spanish.

I Got Lucky (1971). For those disappointed that there was no soundtrack to *Easy Come, Easy Go,* you can now relax.

Elvis Sings Hits from His Movies, Vol. 1 (1972). What hits?

Elvis Singing Flaming Star and Others (1969). Includes "She's a Machine" and "Do the Vega."

Posthumous

Elvis's death rendered him unable to record anymore, but that didn't stop RCA from putting out anything they could find, like 1978's *Canadian Tribute.* Here are the worst:

"The Elvis Medley" (1982). A "Stars on 45" concept, without a common beat to unify the tunes.

I Was the One (1983). Some of the greatest rockabilly of all time, defaced by posthumous overdubs to make it sound more "contemporary." Stupid.

Elvis Aron Presley (1980). An eight-album boxed-set testament to the inability of anyone at RCA to tell the difference between the worthy tracks in their vaults and the duds.

Elvis Sings for Children (and Grownups Too!) (1978). And satisfies neither!

An Elvis Double Feature (1989). After this reissue, it's easy to wonder if compact discs are such a miracle. The set includes songs form *Speedway* and *Clambake,* two of Presley's most desultory pix, including self-explanatory bad tracks like "Who Are You? (Who Am I?)," "Your Groovy Self," and "The Girl I Never Loved."

Major Social Event	Number-One Pop Song	Current Elvis Single
March on Washington August, 1963	Stevie Wonder, "Fingertips"	"Bossa Nova Baby"
Beatles play Sullivan February, 1964	Beatles, "I Want to Hold Your Hand"	"Kissin' Cousins"
War on Poverty bill August, 1964	Supremes, "Where Did Our Love Go?"	"Ask Me"
US troops reach 180,000 December, 1965	Byrds, "Turn! Turn! Turn!"	"Puppet on a String"
Summer of Love June, 1967	Aretha Franklin, "Respect"	"Long-Legged Girl with the Short Dress On"
King assassination April, 1968	Otis Redding, "The Dock of the Bay"	"Stay Away"
Woodstock August, 1969	Rolling Stones, "Honky Tonk Women"	"Clean Up Your Own Back Yard"
U.S. enters Cambodia April, 1970	Jackson Five, "ABC"	"The Wonder of You"

The Fifty Worst Rock-and-Roll Albums of All Time

U2
The Unforgettable Fire
Island, 1984
highest chart position: number twelve

If U2 weren't full of shit, they wouldn't be as great as they often are. Their declared goals are commendable and their songs can ring true at the deepest emotional levels, but the goals they espouse and songs they convey are fueled by a sense of self-importance that would make Sting blush. They think they are the most important band in the world, and sometimes they are. On *The Unforgettable Fire*, they don't even come close.

The Unforgettable Fire is not U2's worst album, but it is the worst album for which we hold them responsible. The 1981 *October* was even messier and more casual—only "Gloria" from that set has lasted—but they were forced by circumstances out of their control to write and record it much too quickly.

The Unforgettable Fire was the follow-up to *War*, a record that U2 singer Bono proudly called "a slap in the face" to complacent listeners. By contrast, *The Unforgettable Fire* was a meek tap on the shoulder. Everything here was implicit; instead of vocals and instruments coming out to greet you, they hid in the background and expected you to listen to the record several dozen times before you discovered them. And they had lots of company in the background, because there was no foreground. The production, by Brian Eno and the usually reliable Daniel Lanois, was as muddy as a South Jersey swamp; when we heard an advance cassette of the record, we were convinced it hadn't yet been mixed. In front of the piled guitars, basses, and drums, there was a big hole where the songs were supposed to be.

Bono's lyrics deepened the hollow. References to such ills as Dublin's heroin problem, the wastes of war, and the assassination of Martin Luther King, Jr., dotted the record, but they were just references, name-dropping. There was no concrete description. Eno's production techniques have always emphasized evasive evocation over straightforward naturalism. He and Lanois never pushed Bono to think out the words that would best serve a song; many of these lyrics sound like improvisations. (The band has since revealed that one, "Elvis Presley & America," is a literal first take.) After the trenchancy of his lyrics to *War*, Bono's refusal to follow through on any of his songwriting ideas was disheartening. "Pride (in the name of love)" was a deeply felt love letter to the ideas of Dr. King and by far the most forthright instrumental track on the LP, but it loses much of its adrenaline rush thanks to Bono's fractured lyric. It's sloppy too: Bono places King's murder in "early morning" instead of the actual late afternoon, probably because the meter worked better that way. Most of the lyrics on this record wouldn't have remained if the band has slept on them overnight. However, no one gave them that much consideration.

At Live Aid and on the tour behind *The Unforgettable Fire*, Bono's stage persona became a joke. Almost immediately, stand-up comics regularly parodied his unnaturally exaggerated gestures and his un-funky formal dancing. Such ridiculous actions drew attention away from the mediocre new material: the show and the commitment were more important than the fact that the songs didn't live up to the between-song slogans. U2 have gone on to make some stirring music and some awkward music, but it's doubtful they'll nap for so long again when they should be making a record.

GRAHAM PARKER AND THE RUMOUR
The Parkerilla
Mercury, 1979
highest chart position: number one hundred and forty-nine

Two of the three studio records Graham Parker and the Rumour recorded for Mercury in the seventies (*Howlin' Wind* and *Heat Treatment*, both from 1976) stand as a pair of rock's most fiery albums. Fronting a large band of pub-rock vets that took its cues from mid-sixties Stax recordings and *St. Dominic's Preview*–period Van Morrison, Parker wrapped his songs in a fury that was undeniably that of a punk rocker. It was remarkable, unprecedented stuff, and for a short time it seemed as if its possibilities were unlimited.

None of Parker's three fine Mercury albums (1977's *Stick to Me* was only a step behind its predecessors) sold in anything approaching significant quantities, and Parker was convinced that the powers at his record label were holding him back: as he sang in "Mercury Poisoning," his later chronicle of the period, "I'm the best-kept secret in the West." Parker gambled that a quickie dud record would get him dropped by Mercury, so he delivered *The Parkerilla*, an indifferent, skimpy fifty-four-minute, double live album that epitomized the concept of a quickie dud. The maneuver worked and Parker promptly moved to Arista, where he debuted with the astonishing *Squeezing Out Sparks.*

The Rumour, built around the interdependent guitars of Martin Belmont and Brinsley Schwarz, normally prodded Parker in the right directions without ever getting in his way, but on *The Parkerilla* they are toned down. Only drummer Steve Goulding seems interested in keeping up the pace; the rest of the band is content to force Parker's agitated songs into relaxation. The nadir of these live performances without many highlights is undoubtedly a funk-free version of "The Heat in Harlem" that goes on for nearly eight minutes before everyone gives up in frustration. The song doesn't go anywhere; 7:35 of the music chasing its own tail drains everyone's already minimal energy.

For Parker's part, either he is practicing for being Foreigner's opening band or he's poorly parodying such a unit. His indecisive patter: "We're gonna try to make this place come crashing down, right?" and "Let's bring some life in here, yeah?" are as assertive and persuasive as this usually articulate man gets. And before you argue that maybe Parker was just so much better on record than he was live that we shouldn't

attack him so harshly, we refer you to *Live at Marble Arch*, an intermittently available promotional LP from a year earlier that scorched every turntable on which it was played.

The live stuff on *The Parkerilla* is bad, but the fourth side is a studio disaster. Some genius decided that Parker's anthemic "Don't Ask Me Questions" would make more sense as a disco single, so they pushed the Rumour into the studio with producer "Mutt" Lange and crossed their fingers. The ominous reggae of the original (on *Howlin' Wind*) was inappropriately accelerated into a more "contemporary" beat, and Lange suffocated the track with an overlay of gimmicky special effects. As Parker hoped, this record—especially the disembowelment of "Don't Ask Me Questions"—was hideous enough to get him dropped, but we'd have been happier if he had found another way to make his move. If Parker wanted to dump his original record company, he could have done it without taking out his anger on his fans. His three good records had been commercial stiffs; chances are a fourth would have been as well.

NICK LOWE
Pinker and Prouder than Previous
Columbia, 1988
highest chart position: did not chart

Why does nearly every rock and roller we trust let us down sooner or later? Elvis, the solo Beatles, the Rolling Stones, the Who—the list is endless. Is it that we hold impossibly high expectations for performers to maintain over the long run, or is rock and roll truly the domain of the young and hungry? At the very least, there is a propensity for performers to start choking on their own fumes once they become rich and famous. Nick Lowe will be the first to tell you he's hardly rich or famous, but for someone who started out with so much promise, he's done more than his share of backsliding.

Lowe first came to the attention of most rock fans as the producer of the decisive early albums by Graham Parker and Elvis Costello. Before that he played bass and wrote country-tinged songs for pub-rock stalwarts Brinsley Schwarz, one of those bands that critics say were great in hindsight but which nobody much liked while they were together. His first two solo albums, *Pure Pop for Now People* (released in the U.K. as *Jesus of Cool*) and *Labour of Lust,* stood as prime examples of the rekindled hope for rock and roll the new British bands represented. Lowe's songs of this period were definitive power pop: infectious melodies coupled with spare, driving arrangements and lyrics that were smart and witty without being self-conscious. Plus you had to like that after David Bowie released his album *Low,* Lowe put out an EP called *Bowi.* Lowe and his band Rockpile helped make real rock and roll smart fun again.

As Rockpile receded into a pleasant memory, Lowe's subsequent recordings returned more and more to the monochromatic country ditties that didn't get any notice when he was with Brinsley Schwarz. By the time he got to *Pinker and Prouder than Previous,* Lowe seemed to have forgotten how to make the kind of rock and roll that had earned him hero status with fans tired of industrial-size rock. On *Pinker and Prouder than Previous* (we hate typing the title as much as you hate reading it), the energetic guitar-based arrangements of Lowe's early albums are gone and we're stuck with the unimaginative keyboard playing of rock-and-roll mercenary Paul Carrack (see also Mike + the Mechanics, "The Living Years," and Roger Waters, *Radio K.A.O.S.*). Carrack's lazy style complements Lowe's bass work, which lopes along, enervating all it touches. In a vain attempt to enliven the songs, ex

Rockpile and sometime Dire Straits drummer Terry Williams—never the most subtle of drummers to begin with (part of his charm, actually)—overplays more than usual.

Disappointing as the music is, Lowe's lyrics are the album's true source of despair (his previous bad albums, *Nick the Knife* and *The Abominable Showman*, were tougher). There's none of the irony of "Cruel to Be Kind." There's no dark humor à la "Marie Provost," a toe-tapper about a real-life silent screen siren who hit the skids when talkies took over and was turned into dog food by her dachshund. As Lowe sang, "She was a winner/That became a doggie's dinner/She never meant that much to me/Oh, poor Marie." Back in the late seventies it seemed he could write a strong, clever song about anything. He once wrote a song about the Bay City Rollers that became a number-one record (in Japan, but it was still a chart-topper). On *Pinker and Prouder than Previous*, we get lyrics like "I've got the love and I'm gonna give it/I've got the love and you're gonna get it./I've got the love and if it don't stop/I'm gonna pop." It's hard to believe these lyrics come from the same man who thought up "I heard they castrated Castro."

Nick Lowe was once quoted as saying that groups like Yes and Genesis are about as exciting as a used Kleenex. (No argument here.) *Pinker and Prouder than Previous* is as disappointing as pulling a used Kleenex out of a pants pocket that you thought had money in it. It's not what you expected, it's useless, and it doesn't feel very good.

SCOTTY MOORE
The Guitar That Changed the World!
Epic, 1964
highest chart position: did not chart

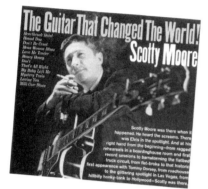

TONY SHERIDAN AND THE ELVIS PRESLEY TCB BAND
Tony Sheridan and the Elvis Presley TCB Band
Cayman Musicorp, 1981
highest chart position: did not chart

No rock and roller cast a longer shadow than Elvis Presley. In the years since Presley died, dozens of rock and country performers have striven either to understand what set Elvis apart or to take unto themselves part of his triumph—which cannot be shared because it was both unprecedented and unrepeatable. Like Buck Brody Mozingo in novelist William Price Fox's *Dixiana Moon*, some have been content to stand back as Elvis shoots by and listen for the deafening ricochet. Others, like Bruce Springsteen in his dark update of Chuck Berry's Elvis parable "Bye, Bye, Johnny," have sought to champion Presley's boldest stroke, the (temporary) destruction of damn near all American musical and cultural barriers. But most merely join in chorus to praise the King.

And then there are those who had an association with Presley and don't have a clue what they should do about it.

Scotty Moore was with Elvis virtually from the start. He was the guitarist and ostensible band leader during Presley's Sun days. He even managed the young Hillbilly Cat for a short spell (alas, he wasn't dexterous enough to keep Colonel Parker's claws off the kid). Along with bassist Bill Black and producer/accidental genius Sam Phillips, he was part of a new sound that nearly forty years later hasn't been surpassed. Moore performed on the soundtracks of many Presley films, and in 1968 he was again part of the definitive Presley sound when he appeared in the "boxing-ring" segment of Elvis's comeback special.

During the sixties, Moore wasn't working full-time for Presley, so he looked for some work on his own and got a solo deal. Hence *The Guitar That Changed the World!,* with a cover that boasted, in a close approximation to the English language: "Scotty Moore was there when it happened. He heard the screams. There was Elvis in the spotlight. And at his right hand from the beginning—from ragged rehearsals in a boardinghouse room and first record session to barnstorming the flatbed truck circuit, from flat-broke to that historic first appearance with Tommy Dorsey, from roadhouse to the glittering spotlight in Las Vegas, from hillbilly honky-tonk to Hollywood, Scotty was there." To underline the association with Presley that was supposed to sell the record, Moore's repertoire for the disc was a dozen familiar songs associated with his once and future boss.

If this was the way Moore wanted the songs to sound from the start, it's a good thing Elvis had the stronger personality. Everything here is soft—even the interchangeable Arthur Crudup tunes "That's All Right" and "My Baby Left Me"—and sweet; Moore played as if the revolution in which he was a high-ranking officer never happened. You're unlikely to find a stronger bunch of rock songs, but you'll never hear them played with any less vigor unless the Mike Curb Congregation reunites. But by 1964 even Elvis had gone soft (sample hit: "Kissin' Cousins"), so this treatment wasn't an anomaly. One good has come out of this record: revisionists who insist that Moore was the genius behind Presley always shut up after they hear it.

It can be argued that, at least subconsciously, *The Guitar That Changed the World!* was an act of revenge by producer Billy Sherrill. Sherrill, whose unforgivably overorchestrated method swamped many great singers (we'll take George Jones without strings, thank you), always considered the Sun sound of Presley and his early labelmates to be primitive hillbilly mess. His own records, he thought, had real class. They had class, all right, but unless they also had a singer strong enough to cut through his mess (we'll cite No-Show Jones again), they didn't have much else. Sherrill always wanted to tame rock and roll; this is as close as he came.

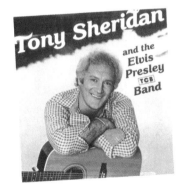

Tony Sheridan is even more of a footnote than Scotty Moore. A British pop crooner briefly backed by the Beatles (his "My Bonnie" is what brought Brian Epstein to the Fabs), Sheridan hasn't done much in the subsequent decades except live off this brief fling with fame.

In 1980 Sheridan once again attracted the attention of a hopeful impresario. Dirk Summer, President of Cayman Musicorp, was belatedly introduced to "My Bonnie" and decided to cut a new record with the legend-by-association. Enlisted as support were members of the TCB ("Taking Care of Business") Band that ably supported Elvis Presley during his Las Vegas and arena-tour years: guitarist James

Burton, pianist Glen D. Hardin (who also produced), drummer Ron Tutt, and bassist *Klaus Voorman?*—Wait a minute! Klaus Voorman? The guy who designed Beatles album covers?

Aside from Voorman (whose parts are replicated by genuine studio bassist Emory Gordy, Jr.), the band plays well, which should be expected since they were able to prop up Elvis musically while he was teetering personally. But even a pilled-up, bloated, self-loathing Elvis is preferable to a Tony Sheridan at the height of his powers. Having failed to pass himself off as the Fifth Beatle (he tried as frequently as Pete Best and almost as blatantly as Murray the K), Sheridan here attempts to become Elvis. As with Moore, his repertoire is based on Elvis-identified tunes ("My Baby Left Me" appears on both records) and unassailable early rock like Buddy Holly's "Rave On" and Chuck Berry's "Johnny B. Goode."

The only problem with Sheridan's singing, aside from limited talent and range, is his penchant for (unconsciously or not) impersonating the original artist. He tries to sound like Carl Perkins when he sings "Blue Suede Shoes," etc. By the end of the record, you wonder if he took lessons from Rich Little. Like *The Guitar That Changed the World!*, *Tony Sheridan and the Elvis Presley TCB Band* proves that any Elvis project without Elvis is likely to fall far short.

DAVID BOWIE
Never Let Me Down
EMI America, 1987
highest chart position: number thirty-four

After he went platinum for the first time in nearly a decade with 1983's *Let's Dance* and supported it with a lengthy tour, David Bowie thought he deserved a break. His 1984 follow-up, *Tonight*, was cut from rough sections of the same cloth as its predecessor, and although its three good songs ("Blue Jean," "Dancing With the Big Boys," "Loving the Alien") were all as slight as a shred of carbon paper, the trio made for pleasant radio listening. Bowie was taking it easy, but the afterburners from *Let's Dance* were powerful enough for him to get away with it.

Bowie's next album made it seem like he worked his ass off on *Tonight*. As a title, *Never Let Me Down* was an unintentional irony; as a record, it barely existed. When you saw the record's first video, "Day-In, Day-Out," which featured Bowie declaiming about urban decay while shuffling by on roller skates, you could tell that Bowie knew the song would get no attention without such ridiculous trappings. The song's stuttering electrobeat sidetracks the proceedings at irregular intervals, and Bowie's chorus—"Day-in, Day-out, Stay-in, Fade-out/Day-in, ooh ooh/Day-in, ooh ooh ooh" (If you find meaning here, please contact us through our publisher)—hammers home that the song is ultimately about nothing, just a series of disconnected images.

When Bowie tries to comment on society in lines like "When you're under the U.S.A./Someone rings a bell and it's all over" (also from "Day-In, Day-Out"), you have to wonder what he's talking about. This lyric recalls Bowie's long-standing inability to understand this country: fourteen years previously he explained the inexplicable "Panic in Detroit" to an interviewer by saying, "There were snipers all over America on tops of buildings, shooting at everybody. That was part of life's rich pattern at the time." There was lots wrong in America in 1973 (the Watergate cover-up, "Tie a Yellow Ribbon 'Round the Old Oak Tree" hitting number one), but we must have missed the full-scale war Bowie saw. Thanks for the news, David.

At least the vocals in "Day-In, Day-Out" sound mildly alert; for the rest of *Never Let Me Down* Bowie sounds like he has just been awoken from an unplanned nap and he's still groggy. We can understand the problem. If we had to sing on a record with Peter Frampton as lead guitarist, we too would have trouble staying awake. Frampton was on

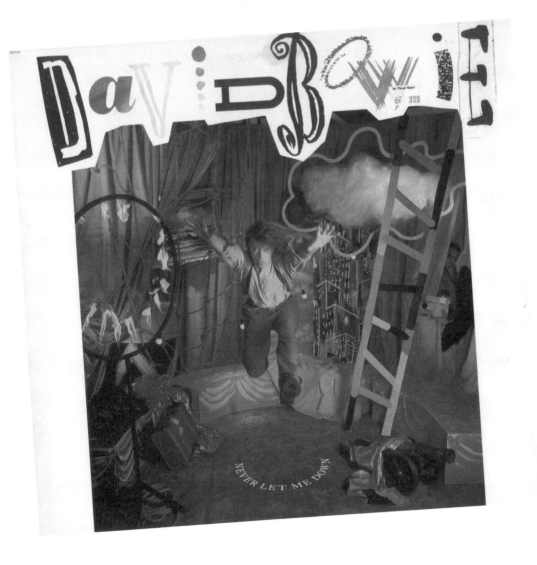

his fourth or fifth failed comeback by 1987 and was lucky to score a gig with his former schoolmate. He sounds like he prepared for *Never Let Me Down* by listening to all the Foreigner records he could find. Even more unfortunate, it sounds like all he listened to on those records were the ballads. The rest of Bowie's band, including the usually excellent guitarist Carlos Alomar, might as well not be there: the heavy-handed electronics push them to the far corner of the mix. Even Iggy Pop's "Bang Bang," a track that demands a stripped-down accompaniment, is drum-machined into mediocrity.

Still, the main culprit here is the man whose name is on the cover. "Glass Spider," the inspiration for the overblown tour of the same name, springs from its opening spoken section: overused lines like "Up until one century ago, there lived, in the Za Duang province of an eastern country, a glasslike spider" seem influenced by Nigel Tufnel's history of the Druids. Bowie may invoke Jacques Brel, Andy Warhol, and Paul Bowles as influences, but this is the first time we've been led to consider Spinal Tap's "Stonehenge" as an antecedent.

Bowie has always been abstruse as a lyricist ("Lady Grinning Soul's cool canasta" from 1973's *Aladdin Sane* is a typical fuzzy image). On *Never Let Me Down*, perhaps because the songs were written quickly, that bleariness brings the words to an all-time low. In "Shining Star (Makin' My Love)," which features an overdramatic rap by intermittently interesting actor and sex symbol to the French Mickey Rourke, we learn that "life is like a broken arrow." Bet you didn't know Bowie was also a philosopher. In "New York's in Life," we discover that "the city grew wings in the back of the night." These are first-draft lyrics and easy rhymes, all sung with such secure self-importance that you can't help giggling like you would at a high-school graduation speech. Feel free to do so. As with such a speaker, Bowie is so wrapped up in his own unformed ideas that he'll never know you're making fun of him.

ELVIS COSTELLO AND THE ATTRACTIONS
Goodbye Cruel World
Columbia, 1984
highest chart position: number thirty-five

Elvis Costello walks into a British record-
ing studio and calls a meeting of his band, the Attractions. "I have some
great new songs," he tells his eager comrades. "They're among the
strongest I've ever written, and they're much more direct and open
than my recent work. If you don't mind, I'm gong to do an acoustic tour
of America and play great versions of these songs."

"Sounds interesting," one Attraction says. "Tell us more."

"I've got a song called 'Peace in Our Time' that really nails political
appeasement both here and in the colonies. And bloody hell, it's as
much an antinuclear anthem as Prince's '1999.' Then there's one called
'Worthless Thing.' It's a love letter to rock and roll and a ransom note
to MTV. You're gonna love it, boys."

Costello pauses briefly to catch his breath and concludes, "These are
very, very special songs to me and I'm quite proud of them."

"Great," the Attractions say as one. "Let's get to work. What shall we
do?"

Costello pulls his glasses to the edge of his nose and scratches the side
of his head before he answers, "You don't understand fellows. I need
your help."

"Your wish is our command."

"Men, you are to help me frame these great songs with the vaguest,
most irrelevant, and most flat-out nonrock arrangements we can find.
We'll be working with the producers Clive Langer and Alan
Winstanley, who proved on our last album that they don't have a clue
how to make us sound like the fierce unit we really are. Please, you
must come as close as possible to rendering these songs inert. If we are
lazy enough, we can make these powerful songs impotent."

And so they did. Costello's ninth album was a profound disappointment to fans who'd heard him play many of its songs during his spring
1984 acoustic tour. Costello, who's no dope, subsequently admitted that
he came close to scrapping the album and replacing it with a solo
acoustic set. Still, *Goodbye Cruel World* indicates that this Bob Dylan
fan identified so deeply with his role model that he wanted to put out

his own album-length rant of self-loathing, his own *Self-Portrait*. All you can hear on this record is distance: distance between Costello and his band, between Costello and his material, between Costello and his audience.

Costello promptly regained his status as one of the eighties' most important performers—his 1986 albums *King of America* and *Blood and Chocolate* rank among his finest—but even diehard fans like us came away from *Goodbye Cruel World* wondering if it really was a suicide note for his career.

VARIOUS PERFORMERS
"Sgt. Pepper's Lonely Hearts Club Band The Original
Soundtrack to the Motion Picture"
RSO, 1978

highest chart position: number five

Recipe for disaster:

- Bring together Peter Frampton and the Bee Gees, two of the biggest-selling acts of the mid-seventies, not to mention some of the most frequently boring superstars of the time. Frampton's break-through album, the ironically titled *Frampton Comes Alive*, owed much of its success to the fact that the diminutive guitarist had long hair and looked good with his shirt open; the has-been Bee Gees had reemerged by piggybacking onto the ascendance of disco. Both were impressive marketing successes; both were musically irrelevant.

- Bring together Dee Anthony, Frampton's manager, and Robert Stigwood, the Bee Gees' shepherd, both egomaniacs known for overexposing their clients for quick bucks. Make them both think they're running the show.

- Base the movie's music on the Beatles' landmark *Sgt. Pepper's Lonely Hearts Club Band*, an album that had already yielded too many cover versions, many of them bad.

- Try to weave the songs on *Sgt. Pepper*, as well as a dozen-odd other late-period Beatles tunes, none of which have any narrative links, into a coherent story.

- Cast George Burns as Mr. Kite and ask him to sing "Fixing a Hole."

- Cast Steve Martin as Dr. Maxwell Edison and ask him to sing "Maxwell's Silver Hammer." (Clever, no?)

- Do all this without the participation of any of the Beatles.

- Do this *with* the participation of Billy Preston, a sideman fresh from helping the Rolling Stones sound feeble.

- Keep a straight face when you explain all this to the media.

- Ignore the lessons of the overblown, underthought film version of the Who's rock opera *Tommy* (which at least had something resembling a storyline).

- Ask Frampton and the Brothers Gibb to act.

- Expect them to act.

- Hire the members of Toto, just in case Frampton's band can't cut it. (By now we're reduced to talking about members of Toto playing Beatles songs behind Peter Frampton and the Bee Gees.)

- On the inner sleeve to the soundtrack, give the Bee Gees the following credit: "vocals for special effects."

- Conduct "additional recording" at four studios, proving that no one has any clue what to do. In desperation, bring in Beatles producer George Martin and Beatles engineer Geoff Emerick. Cross your fingers.

- Perform versions of the Beatles chestnuts with thin vocals and overorchestrated backups, so there's no way the performances can't be considered unintentional parodies.

It was doomed from the start. Beatles fans are excused for hoping that when the Sex Pistols toured around the time this album was made, they came armed with guns, not guitars.

PHANTOM, ROCKER, AND SLICK
Phantom, Rocker, and Slick
EMI America, 1986
highest chart position: number forty-one

Mediocre talent on its own is just dull; a partnership of mediocre talents can generate something truly awful.

Once and future Stray Cats Jim Phantom and Lee Rocker mated with former David Bowie guitarist Earl Slick in 1985 and gave birth to a flash-rock supergroup that aimed for the lowest common denominator. They succeeded completely. The singing by bassist Lee Rocker (real name: Leon Drucker) was surprisingly good considering he was not the lead singer in the Stray Cats (fluent guitarist Brian Setzer was), and Phantom's drumming was terse and dramatic. But the songs they performed had even less originality than the Stray Cats' most blatant rockabilly retreads.

Phantom, Rocker, and Slick's musical and lyrical concerns were an unintentional parody of the worst parts of album-oriented radio (AOR), which was going through a particularly vacuous period. Throughout the album, Phantom, Rocker, and Slick share with us how difficult it is to be rock stars. These poor men, it seems, have to play for less-than-ideal audiences ("Sing for Your Supper"), work two long hours each day ("Time on My Hands"), suffer the wrath of critics ("Men Without Shame"), and make lots of money ("Hollywood Distractions"). Eye-opening, no?

Moreover, these tales of woe are filled with long Slick guitar solos that nullify any excitement that may have inadvertently entered the mix. Even "My Mistake," the one time the trio comes close to sounding honest, eventually deteriorates into a showcase for Slick's guitar techniques and adds another credit to his résumé of failures.

At the same time, Setzer was putting together his own solo record, *The Knife Feels Like Justice*, which was a broad, exhilarating break from the confines of his former group. Unfortunately, that and a follow-up both stiffed badly. After a second stiffed album of their own, Phantom and Rocker skulked back to the Stray Cats. Slick has not been able to talk Bowie into taking him back.

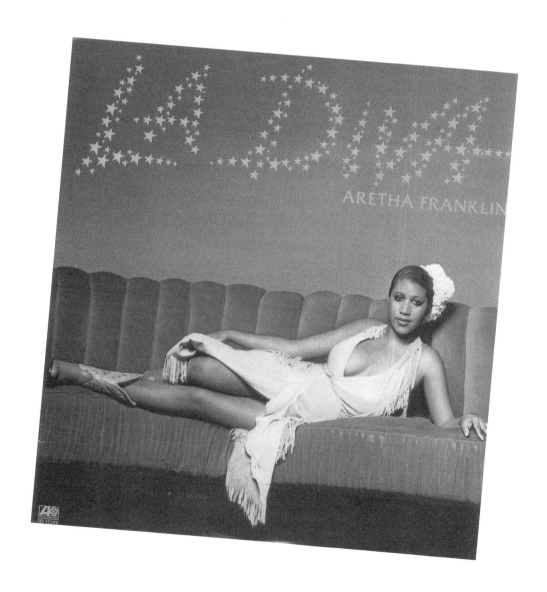

ARETHA FRANKLIN
La Diva
Atlantic, 1979

highest chart position: number one hundred and forty-six

Blame disco. For every worthwhile new singer it uncovered, like Donna Summer, it ruined the careers of one hundred soul and blues singers. On *La Diva*, released at the height of disco insanity, Lady Soul's number gets called.

By 1979, it had been five years since Aretha had scored a Top Ten pop single and seven years since her last Top Ten pop album (the R&B charts, however, had been kinder). After 1972's *Amazing Grace*, her last great album and her final collaboration with producer Jerry Wexler, she had gone through several big-name producers (Quincy Jones, Curtis Mayfield, and Lamont Dozier), none of whom were able to elicit from Franklin the magnificent performances that were once second nature. Van McCoy, the creator of "The Hustle," was a logical next stop on her tour of producers. Unfortunately, it was a dead end: the record wasn't any good, nearly no one bought it, and within a year Franklin had moved on to another label.

The main problem with *La Diva* is not so much that it is wretched (though, of course, it is) as that it is a submediocre disco outing by a truly great vocal stylist who has no business wasting her time this way. One can't help but come away with the impression that Aretha and Atlantic, desperate for a hit, were trying to cash in on the latest trend— something Franklin had never resorted to before, even when her early Columbia singles bombed on the pop charts. It is obvious that Franklin's massive talents are ill-used in a form in which the beat is far more important than conveying emotion in a vocal.

Franklin, who once wrote love songs as complex and irrefutable as any, sank to the floor on *La Diva* with lines like "I'm gonna be the only star tonight on the dance floor" and "We're disco queens/We're really outta sight" (from "Only Star," which further deteriorates into "Qué pasa" chants). Aretha singing disco is as sensible as her posing seductively on the cover in a low-cut dress and cowboy boots . You try hitting the floor at Studio 54 with those and see what happens. The unimaginative production from McCoy and cohort Charles Kipps regurgitates the obvious disco moves of the day: this could be any of McCoy's studio groups. What makes *La Diva* irredeemable is that it offers nothing distinctively Aretha: there's nothing remotely soulful about it.

RINGO STARR
Stop and Smell the Roses
Boardwalk, 1981
highest chart position: number ninety-eight

RINGO STARR
Old Wave
RCA (Canada), 1983
highest chart position: did not chart

At the end of the first side of his worst album, *Stop and Smell the Roses*, formerly interesting ex-Beatle Ringo Starr says, "I'm going crazy with this record business. I want to stop it. You want me to stop it."

So why didn't he stop? Apart from a fine 1971 single ("It Don't Come Easy" b/w "Early 1970") and 1973's *Ringo*, a funny, warm, off-the-wall set that featured Richard Perry's everything-including-the-kitchen-sink overproduction as well as contributions from his former bandmates, Starr has stumbled from disaster to disaster. He has tried everything: a country album, a record of pop standards, half a dozen sets that tried to replicate *Ringo*. The nadir came when Starr went to court to prevent the release of songs recorded in Memphis with Chips Moman, afraid that the resulting album would lose him whatever remaining goodwill he could still count on. Starr didn't hit paydirt until 1989, when he gave up on making records, announced he was no longer a drunk, and assembled a band of well-known players (at least one of whom also announced that he was no longer a drunk) to back him on a nostalgia tour.

In 1981 Ringo got *Stop and Smell the Roses* released in America, barely (a small independent label put it out); by the time *Old Wave* leaked out of the studio two years later, it stunk so badly that no American record company would touch it. The last cut on *Smell* is a lifeless remake of "Back Off Boogaloo," a more assertive version of which had been a hit for the former drummer in 1972. As if the embarrassment of having to cover one's own decade-old hit to provide a climax for a miserable record isn't sad enough, this version ends with Ringo and his drinking buddies warbling random lines from Beatles songs. This is Ringo's admission that no one would notice his current work were it not for his past. He went one better on *Old Wave*, going back even further by putting a pre-Beatles photo of himself on its cover. Perhaps if Ringo had continued to record, his next album would have been emblazoned with a cover of Mrs. Starkey while she was pregnant with little Richard.

Smell exuded a minor hit in "Wrack My Brain" (number thirty-eight), written and produced by George Harrison, who like all surviving ex-Beatle songsmiths, had no musical ideas in the early eighties that weren't tributes to John. Aside from being amused by hearing Starr bellow, "I'm all dried-up" (no kidding), we also get to hear George rhyme *brain* with *pain, rain, game*(?), *lane,* and of course, *insane.* Ah, songwriting. Fellow dried-up ex-mop-top Paul McCartney shows up to write and produce several songs that are most distinguished by wife Linda's thin background vocals and lines like "My philosophy/Don't go fooling with private property" and "Come on baby, give it all you've got./Get into the power of the plot." Oh. Harry Nilsson contributes "Drumming Is My Madness," which neither is mad nor includes much noticeable drumming (what stickwork is apparent is provided by studio ace Jim Keltner).

For *Old Wave,* Ringo found a new pal, former Eagles guitarist Joe Walsh. This alliance resulted in a collection that rocked somewhat harder than *Smell* but still had the misfortune of being built around an over-the-hill entertainer who had lost his interest in drumming and no longer worked to charm audiences with his off-key, rangeless singing. With lyrics like "They win and they lose/They pick and they choose" to put across, perhaps Starr figured it wasn't worth the effort.

The problem with rocking up the material on *Old Wave* is that Starr isn't up to it. Once again he has other drummers shadowing him, and he can't get by with the same genial deadpan in his monotonic vocals that he uses on his lighter efforts. Not that Walsh gives him much room. On "Be My Baby" (alas, a Walsh original), the producer's incessant wah-wah effects make it sound like he's strangling someone (or maybe it's just the sound Walsh makes when he wakes up). With all that six-string screaming, there's no room for modest-voiced Ringo. Other inappropriate touches clutter the record, like the ersatz Dixieland horns Walsh invokes to shut down a cover of the Sir Douglas Quintet's "She's About a Mover."

The truest moment on *Old Wave* comes during a slump through Chuck Jackson's 1962 hit "I Keep Forgettin'." When Ringo sings, "I keep forgettin' you don't love me no more./I keep forgettin' you don't want me no more," he's singing to his audience, even if he doesn't know it. He hasn't released a record of new material since.

AMERICA
History/America's Greatest Hits
Warner Bros., 1975
highest chart position: number three

We thought we'd been spared. Although Crosby, Stills, and Nash polluted the landscape with their early seventies mush, they spent so much time arguing ("No, Stephen, your solo has to fit on one side of the record.") they didn't get around to recording much. But those of you who weren't napping during high-school science class remember that every void needs to be filled. Denny Bunnell, Gerry Beckley, and Dan Peek were the unwelcome fillers of that void, but what they came up with was so vacant they might as well not have bothered.

Bunnell, Beckley, and Peek made up America (actually, Vespucci's apologists made up America, but that's another book), one of those soft-rock bands of the seventies that frequently couldn't even work up enough energy to be mellow. They had a career defined by frequent purchases of rhyming dictionaries and an all-around dumbness epitomized by their violation of the United Nations cultural boycott of South Africa. They deserved to be where they were a decade later, opening concerts for Christopher Cross. Naming a band America is another act of phenomenal dumbness, although it does result in amusing credits like "all other instruments and vocals by America." That narrows it down.

You still don't believe they're dumb? Well, what if we told you the band thought it was clever to start the title of seven consecutive albums with the letter *H?* We thought that would quiet you down.

Their first hit was "A Horse with No Name," a "Heart of Gold" sound-alike that has more to do with Neil Young's three bandmates (C, S, and N) than anything Young himself might come up with. Randy Newman, always good for a zinger, once called "A Horse with No Name" a song "about a kid who thinks he's taken acid." With lines like "In the desert you can remember your name"—is it so hard elsewhere?—the rule, we can't argue. America didn't rip off only Americans; Brits got swiped as well. "I Need You" bears more than a passing resemblance to the Beatles' "Something," a noncoincidence accentuated by the contribution of Beatles producer George Martin to the track. Perhaps Martin figured he made "Something" sound good once and didn't want to mess with what worked. Either that, or he'd accept work with *anybody.* The guitar line in "Sister Golden Hair" also screams George Harrison,

and lyrics like "Will you meet me in the middle/Will you meet me in the air?" (we can definitely say this band is not grounded) are just as lazily cosmic as those that suffused the two decades of Harrison's career between the Beatles and the Wilburys.

Bad lyrics jump out at you and make you wish they hadn't printed the words on the inner sleeve. In "Ventura Highway," we see "alligator lizards in the air" and find our heroes "wishin' on a falling star/Watchin' for the early train./Sorry, boy, but I've been hit by purple rain." (We hope this isn't where Prince got the idea.) In "Tin Man," America sings, "Sometimes late when things are real." In "Only in Your Heart," we learn that "life gets so hard when you reach the end" (?) and are confronted with a weird heavy-metal coda (it really does get hard at the end) that suggests a cold-turkey version of Iron Butterfly.

We can't forget 1973's "Muskrat Love." Their depiction of love between muskrats Suzie and Sam straddles the line between mellow and psychedelic (that is, it's boring *and* pretentious), but let's face it: America (the band) was just too far ahead of its time. By 1976, America (the country) was finally ready for a hit version from the Captain and Tennille. That's called progress. History is supposed to be about progress, but this *History* is about repeating the same mistakes over and over.

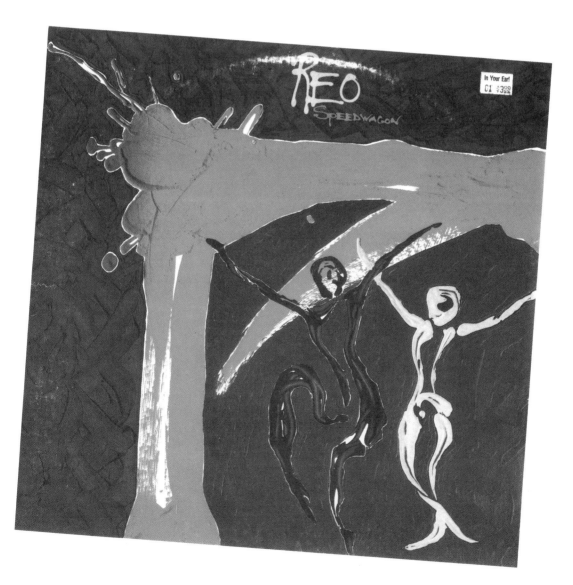

REO SPEEDWAGON
Life as We Know It
Epic, 1987
highest chart ranking: number twenty-eight.

On *Life as We Know It,* the bland-rock group REO Speedwagon grasped at maturity and fell down so hard all you could hear was us laughing. On the surface, this ostensibly ambitious move made sense: after a dozen-odd albums of peppy midtempo love songs and rockers, the permanently adolescent group must have wanted to try something new, if only from platinum boredom. But, like teenagers, REO Speedwagon acted as if starting anew were a simple process that could be completed by pushing the right buttons. The band called in the crack songwriting team of Tom Kelly and Bill Steinberg (they wrote "Like a Virgin" for Madonna and "True Colors" for Cyndi Lauper and let the latter become a film commercial over Lauper's objections); the team's cliché-filled contributions to this album are virtually indistinguishable from those by REO Speedwagon lead singer Kevin Cronin. REO Speedwagon also upped the grit factor a smidgen in the arrangements and started singing about bad times as much as good times. They were convinced this would yield an instant breakthrough.

But *Life as We Know It* replaced one used-up formula with another that was immediately spent. Many of the numbers were about long-term relationships gone sour, with titles like "New Way to Love," "Variety Tonight," and "Tired of Getting Nowhere." Most distressing were the Kelly-Steinberg contributions, especially the hyperactive "Over the Edge" (cowritten with REO Speedwagon guitarist Gary Richarath), which sounds painfully like the title tune to *Footloose.* Kelly and Steinberg's work for Madonna and Cyndi Lauper seemed detailed and honest; the songs here were just plain embarrassing. If this is life as we know it, then perhaps ignorance is bliss.

JOEL GREY
Black Sheep Boy
Columbia, 1969
highest chart position: did not chart

Everybody wants to be hip. As a teen-
ager, Joel Grey was a protégé of Eddie Cantor and developed enough
singing, dancing, theatrical, and impressionist skills to get himself
booked as a headliner at the Copa. Throughout the sixties he appeared
in a variety of Broadway plays and national theatrical tours. Eventually,
in 1972, he became a true star when he reprised his Broadway role as
the Master of Ceremonies in the film version of *Cabaret*.

But in 1969, the prestar Grey was in a quandary. He didn't enjoy what
he was doing on Broadway (joining shows as a midrun replacement,
kind of like Paul Carrack) and didn't feel his work was especially
relevant to the music he loved. We'll let Grey tell the story: "I've always
had a kind of private person inside that this album is a reflection of.
This music has always been an important part of my life, especially the
poetic aspects of contemporary lyrics."

Like many nonrock entertainers before and after (ever hear Robert
Goulet's "Both Sides Now"?), Grey was drawn to rock and roll (or at
least folk rock) and wanted to be part of it. Hence his album *Black
Sheep Boy*. But don't consider the record a mere sellout move
(although there is something rather amusing about the idea of selling
out by making a rock record). Grey is remarkably earnest here—in the
liner notes rock critic wanna-be Grey calls the Beatles' "Ob-La-Di, Ob-
La-Da" a "kind of a crazy, West Indian vaudeville turn"—but a pure
heart does not mean a good record. If *Black Sheep Boy* was just
another example of a confused stage actor trying to rock, it would be
nothing special. The record's earnestness is what makes it truly rank.

You know you're in trouble as soon as the needle drops on the first
track, Tim Hardin's "If I Were a Carpenter." Grey is still on a
Broadway stage here, using broad vocal gestures to put over dubious
lines (and face it, this folk-rock standard has loads of those). The simple
bass-swooping arrangement is soon augmented by silly orchestra-pit
strings and woodwinds, enhancing the song's melodramatic aspects
and encouraging Grey to emote so hard you can almost hear the blood
vessels bulging on his forehead. He believes! On "Scarborough Fair/
Canticle," which he describes as "like a twelfth-century troubadour,
and yet there's something timeless and totally contemporary," he tries
to find meaning in Paul Simon's overrated rip-off of "North Country

Girl" by stretching out notes so long he forgets what word he's singing. And after hearing his version of Cream's "White Room," we don't expect to see any "Joel Is God" posters.

Grey's covers of Joni Mitchell and Donovan tunes have even less substance than the originals, although it sounds like he cares more for the songs than the writers did. On *Black Sheep Boy*, Grey is a folk-rock zealot, and he has all the naive enthusiasm of a recent convert: *you* try to get excited about "Jennifer Juniper" and see how far you get. Still, he can't escape his past: he sings everything like a theatrical showstopper. At the end of each track he sounds disappointed that there's no applause.

Grey saves the worst for the Beatles covers at the end of each side. His performance on a staccato "She's Leaving Home" (opening and closing with an ominous church gong) bastardizes the tale into a nascent New Age be-all-you-can-be slogan. Grey overdubs his own harmonies, singing so intensely and incorrectly that you hope he gets run over by the man at the motor trade. The record crashes to a conclusion with "Ob-La-Di, Ob-La-Da." It's done as novelty, a Borscht Belt version of "Puff the Magic Dragon" the bluehairs of all ages can sing along with. Grey is completely out of his element here, trying to prove he is contemporary by turning a substandard Beatles tune—redeemed only by its energy—into a version one could imagine Merv Griffin replicating. Life may be a cabaret, old chum, but this is not living.

STARLAND VOCAL BAND
4 × 4

Windsong, 1980

highest chart position: are you kidding?

You'll notice that nowhere in this book have we talked about some of the truly wretched performers who usually pop up in even the most perfunctory conversation about the worst records. Nothing about the Carpenters, no snide comments about John Denver, barely a mention of the Captain and Tennille. Who wants to read a book about Terry Jacks's "Seasons in the Sun"? We could try to convince you that this is because our parents raised us to be somewhat respectful of others, but after all the stuff we've been saying about David Crosby, we don't think you'll buy that. We decided from the beginning that we weren't going to concentrate on these performers; nobody who really cares about rock and roll expects much from them anyway, and besides, the publisher ain't paying us near enough to sit through the whole Carpenters catalog and try to ferret out their very worst album.

But in the course of our research we came across one such album that we just couldn't resist.

The Starland Vocal Band was a quartet of laid-back studio hack singers who somehow (booster John Denver's name recognition? that dumb pedal-steel line? payola?) managed to score a number-one hit in 1976 with a sophomoric double entendre about making love during the day, the wretched "Afternoon Delight." Not recognizing their status as lucky one-hit wonders, the band turned this unfortunate lapse of judgment by record buyers into a summer television variety series and the chance to record even more insipid songs showcasing their vapid harmonies.

Their album *4 × 4* represents the nadir of seventies easy-listening pap pop, as you could probably tell without even putting the record on the turntable. Any album whose cover features one of the band members wearing a white leisure suit with an open-collared shirt and gold chains hanging from his neck and on which a swami is thanked in the liner notes belongs at the bottom of the barrel.

We'd like to say that these are the most inane songs we've ever heard, but to do that we'd have to grant that these qualify as complete songs. Half-baked ideas like "Apartment for Rent," "Baby Sent a Letter," and "Down at the Hop" are all chorus and bridge with no real verses. Of course, when you try to write a verse and come up with "Maybe today will be yesterday's fun/Maybe tomorrow is under our thumb./We'll go for the minute instead of the mile/Then again maybe we won't even run," you're probably better off sticking with the chorus.

All right, so the originals aren't any good. Give them the benefit of the doubt, somebody out there is saying (anybody?); these people are professional backup singers, not songwriters. How do they do on the cover versions of Bob Dylan's "You're Gonna Make Me Lonesome When You Go" and Ike Turner's "A Fool in Love"? "A Fool in Love" is given the typical Starland Vocal Band treatment: rather than let any single member take the lead line, arrange the song for four voices. It might do wonders for group harmony (you know that one was coming), but it sure doesn't do anything for the song. "You're Gonna Make Me Lonesome When You Go" is another matter entirely. Not only does the group drag out every word in a torturous effort to make it fit their depressurized harmonies, but they give the music a bounce that hasn't been so out of place since Pat Boone's version of "Ain't That a Shame."

The ultimate insult comes with their version of "La Bamba," here titled "Everybody La Bamba" and featuring "new lyrics" by Bill Danoff and Jonathan Caroll (two of the Vocal Bandits) and great keyboardist/ apparently indiscriminate producer Barry Beckett. See, when you take a song that's in the public domain and add something new to it—not something good, just something slightly different—you can copyright it in your name and collect royalties. Why else would anyone take this rock-and-roll classic and add lines like "Down in old Alabama/In Muscle Shoals, Alabama/We sing this song/And we learned it from Ana." Ana? Ah, who cares? "Everybody La Bamba" sums up 4×4: the singing is all the kind of thin harmony that characterizes careers spent in the studio providing backing tracks on real songs, the song itself is just about all chorus, and the new lyrics are on a par with those a grade-schooler would make up off the top of his head after hearing the song once on the radio.

In their stage show, noted background singers Flo and Eddie used to do a medley of the hit songs that they had provided the harmonies on. But instead of singing full renditions of the songs, they would "oooh" and "aaah" when the band got to the chorus of "Bang a Gong" or "Hungry Heart." Too bad the Starland Vocal Band didn't realize what Flo and Eddie did: background singers should be heard, but only in small snatches.

EMERSON, LAKE, AND PALMER
Tarkus
Cotillion, 1971
highest chart position: number nine

How out of control were the egos of keyboardist Keith Emerson, guitarist Greg Lake, and drummer Carl Palmer in the seventies? Let's examine the evidence:

● Their 1974 live album *Welcome back, my friends, to the show that never ends, Ladies and Gentlemen, Emerson, Lake, and Palmer* had to be extended to a triple album to accommodate all three members' megalomaniacal desires for solo space. We know Yes did the same thing on their interminable *Yessongs*, but at least there were five of them.

● All three members had so little use for each other's ideas that they went nearly four years between studio albums.

● When they finally did get around to putting out a new album, 1977's double LP *Works, Volume 1*, they only worked together on two songs, one of them a bizarre dismemberment of Aaron Copland's "Fanfare for the Common Man." Each of the three other sides of the double album was given to one of the members. No one worked on anyone else's side.

● Eight months later, they put out *Works, Volume 2*, a single LP of outtakes from the first volume. Again, most of the material on this record was solo.

● A year later, still bickering, they put out *Love Beach (Love Beach?)* another LP comprising primarily solo ideas that weren't strong enough to make it onto previous records. Then they broke up. So their last two albums were essentially outtakes from the previous album, which itself was mostly solo material. In other words, Emerson, Lake, and Palmer didn't truly record as a group for the final five of their eight years.

The other three years produced pretentious mush. Their outlandish complaints to the contrary, there never was and never will be such a thing as classical rock. All the hallmarks of great "serious" music—among them precise arrangement for large orchestras, esoteric themes, and lengthy compositions—are usually anathema to rock and roll. But none of the three stooges in Emerson, Lake, and Palmer has a commitment to either classical music or rock and roll. They'll plunder

Bach, Bernstein, and Berry with equal nonchalance and equal misunderstanding. ELP's albums are suffused with the attitude that their ideas were far more important than those of their sources and that these silly little men, like Mussorgsky and Tchaikovsky, should be grateful that pseudorock gods were ripping them off.

Although they later deteriorated into a joke of proportions epic enough to be worthy of their pretensions, the foibles of Emerson, Lake, and Palmer were never so apparent as on their second album, *Tarkus*. Less than a minute into the record you hear your first gong shot, which should signal what is going to happen. Emerson's organ is the lead instrument on the record, but it is Lake's hilarious lyrics that hold sway. In just the first song he lets loose with "Have the days made you so unwise?", "Will you know how the seed is sown?", and "How can you talk to the winds of time?" With questions like this, Lake should be in a remedial poetry class.

Tarkus must be a rock opera, at least the first side, which is all one song (names of the sections: Eruption, Stones of Years, Iconoclast, Mass, Manticore, Battlefield, and Aquatarkus). We say "must be" because we're not sure. There's a picture of ol' Tarkus on the cover. He appears to be a giant armadillo with the body of a tank. The story never gels in the songs, but thanks to painter William Neal, the gatefold sleeve is chock full of images that supposedly tell the story. It looks like Tarkus exploded out of a volcano, fought several fellow combination animal/battle vehicles, and eventually skipped town. But your guess is as good as ours. These scenes must correspond with the few dramatic sections on the side. We know they're dramatic because the pace quickens for a bit and Lake yells his inane questions a little louder. Tarkus represents something (technology? nature? a rat that once bit Greg in the ankle?), but this symbolism is too obscure.

Side two doesn't even try to cohere—*you* find a way to unite "Bitches Crystal" and "Infinite Space (Conclusion)"—and in its final track, "Are You Ready Eddy?" (apparently directed at recording engineer Eddy Offord), Emerson, Lake, and Palmer make a brief, awkward attempt to rock out. Lake sings as if he thinks echo will compensate for energy, Palmer doesn't play fast enough, so the pace drags, and Emerson of course can't stop soloing, dropping in obvious classical licks and lines from show tunes. "Are you ready to rock and roll?" Lake howls over and over. Eddy might be, Greg, but you'll never be.

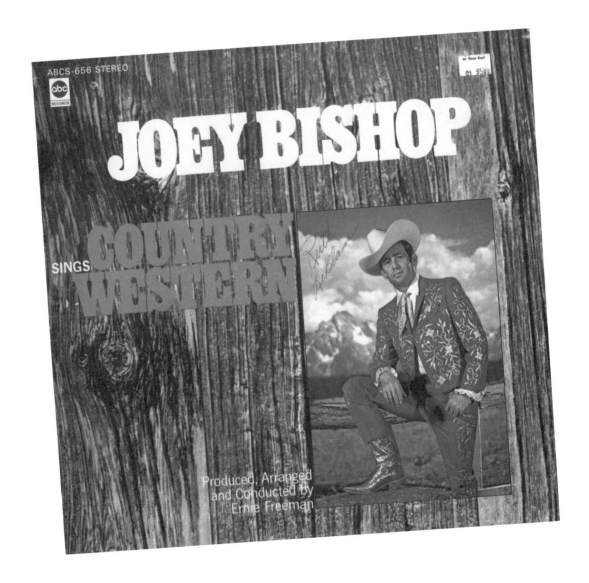

JOEY BISHOP
Joey Bishop Sings Country Western
ABC, 1968

highest chart position: did not chart outside of Las Vegas

At this point we'd like to recommend *Golden Throats: The Great Celebrity Sing-Off*, a wonderful compilation album Rhino Records put out in 1988. It includes popular songs of the sixties ("Proud Mary," "Like a Rolling Stone," etc.) as attempted over the years by actors-who-wanted-to-sing like Eddie Albert, Sebastian Cabot, Joel Grey, Andy Griffith, Jim Nabors, Leonard Nimoy, William Shatner, Jack Webb, and Mae West. The record is a splendid horror, a joy for those who revel in bad pop, and an (unheeded) warning to future television stars to not get above their raising. Philip-Michael Thomas, don't you pay attention to anything?

One of the most bizarre of such attempts—and one of the few colossally bad ones of the sixties not included in *Golden Throats*—was deadpan comedian Joey Bishop's attempt to become a country music star. Bishop was a minor member of Frank Sinatra's infamous Rat Pack and was also known as a second-rate Borscht Belt comic and failed late-night TV talk show host. ABC Television featured him in one of their periodic attempts to unseat Johnny Carson. They should have known from the start that "The Joey Bishop Show" was doomed to failure: on the first show, guest Ronald Reagan showed up late and another guest, Debbie Reynolds, injured announcer Regis Philbin while showing how to help someone who is on fire. The only thing in flames that night in April 1967 was Bishop's television career. Not only were his jokes deadpan, but so was his audience.

Probably still under contract to ABC, Bishop moved to their records division. Figuring that his buddies Frank, Sammy, and Dino had the pop-schlock field cornered, he decided to take on country schlock. As Ernie Freeman writes on the back cover of *Joey Bishop Sings Country Western*, Joey "approached this album with the same intensity and search for perfection that he brings to his comedy." Alas, this is true. And since apologist Freeman is credited as the producer, arranger, and conductor of the record—and as such probably had points on it—it was in his interest to perpetuate the lie that this was a genuine country record.

Although Bishop predates Kinky Friedman as the original Texas Jewboy, there is nothing outrageous about this album, nothing to indicate that someone known for his alleged sense of humor is the featured artist. Bishop is simply ill-suited for vocalizing. His voice isn't merely soft; once it touches a word, it evaporates. His off-key singing has zero presence; it sounds like he had so much trouble reading the words on the cue cards that he never got a chance to figure out what the songs meant. And with the responsibility of singing some of the greatest country songs ever (most of them written by or associated with Hank Williams), you can't get by putting them across in a narcotized fashion. Freeman's ridiculously overblown arrangements (he makes Billy Sherrill seem like Swamp Dogg) don't cloak Bishop's ineptitude. Instead, because there are massive holes in the mix for Bishop's voice, they just augment the nonsinger's nontalent.

It's hard to tell these ten songs apart, but there is no moment more bizarre than the one at the end of "Your Cheatin' Heart" when Bishop drops his high-register whisper and speaks, "Nobody likes a cheatin' chick," trying to take a Sinatra-style ad lib. Not only does this mean-spirited comment (he all but spits the words; it's the only alive moment on the whole album) come out of nowhere—it has no relation to the song—but it exemplifies how Bishop's smarmy, Vegas/Hollywood attitude has no relation to the honesty of Hank-style country. *Joey Bishop Sings Country Western* is a record about Bishop's ego. I'm such a star, he thinks, I can get away with anything. I'm more important than these stupid hillbilly songs. Forget that I can't sing—I'm Joey Bishop!

DONOVAN
Donovan's Greatest Hits
Epic, 1969
highest chart position: number four

Released at the peak of the wan singer's popularity, *Donovan's Greatest Hits* contains all the songs that made this fey Scotsman the darling of the hippie movement. Such credentials necessitate his inclusion here.

When Donovan first appeared on the scene, the music industry—particularly in Britain—regarded him as little more than a second-rate Bob Dylan imitator. He had all the trappings of a New Dylan: he sported the requisite common-man denim outfit including engineer's cap, he wore a harmonica rack around his neck, and he carried around an acoustic guitar that bore three-quarters of the slogan that Dylan's idol Woody Guthrie had scrawled on his axe a quarter century before (Donovan's read "This machine kills," leaving off the key last word of Guthrie's original, "fascists").

One of our favorite moments from any rock-and-roll movie that isn't *This Is Spinal Tap* occurs in *Don't Look Back*, D. A. Pennebaker's fake cinema-verité study of Dylan's 1964 British tour. During a party in Dylan's hotel suite attended by fired Animal Alan Price, passé folk popularizer Joan Baez, and assorted hangers-on of even less importance (imagine), we see Donovan singing some nondescript song to the small group. Dylan then asks if he can borrow the guitar and proceeds to sing the most venomous version possible of "It's All Over Now, Baby Blue." After the song, the camera zooms in on Donovan, outclassed and completely forgotten by the rest of the party. From the gaping silence that separates true genius from derivative hack, he pipes up, "I used to know a girl named Baby Blue." No one cares.

Donovan soon chucked the folkie act. If the run-in with Dylan wasn't enough to convince him to make the move, the horrible U.S. chart showing of his single "Colours" should have done the trick. Whatever the reason, Donovan hooked up with producer Mickie Most, who had previously worked with the Animals (for which we give him credit) and Herman's Hermits (which immediately wipes away that credit), changed record labels (new sound, new advance), and latched onto the latest countercultural rage: psychedelia.

It was a perfect match: "Sunshine Superman," his first single after the metamorphosis, reached number one. The gentle nature and boyish charm that Donovan projected through his wispy voice caught the emerging hippie ideals of promoting peace and love toward all beings in the universe who aren't square and setting yourself free from the conventions of society that you disagree with this week. Simple as paper, "Sunshine Superman" was designed to appeal to the little kid inside every flower child.

"Mellow Yellow," the follow-up to "Sunshine Superman," is the lyrical equivalent of a Rorschach test. The verses are splotched together, and the song is sung with such nasal detachment that it can mean whatever you want it to. This was perfect for Donovan's core audience: most of them were usually so stoned they could find cosmic messages in just about anything, especially the verse about the "electrical banana." What an inspiration! If you dry out some banana peels and smoke them, you'll get a great high.

Yeah, right. Sounding more like a be-in accidentally recorded than a bona fide song, "Mellow Yellow" is also notable in that it marks the first appearance by Paul McCartney on one of the worst records ever recorded. (There would be many, many more.)

Donovan's Greatest Hits contains all his acoustic-guitar-and-wood-wind-based singles and even takes a passing nod (albeit in rerecorded form) at his pre-flower-power career. The two songs, "Catch the Wind" (as in "Blowin' in...") and "Colours," are naturally not political tunes but sub-Dylan love songs. On the new version of "Colours," Donovan whispers the entire record's only trenchant line, "Freedom is a word that I rarely use without thinking," as if he wasn't thinking about it at all. As long as the money was right, Donovan was ready to go from politically aware to willfully naive.

When advertisers first started to catch on to the idea of using familiar pop hits to push product, one of the first artists whose catalogue was made available was hippie spokesman Donovan. His "Wear Your Love Like Heaven" sold shampoo; "Mellow Yellow" became a soft drink. More will undoubtedly follow. Imagine "Jennifer Juniper" perfume, "Sunshine Superman" window cleaner. These deals will allow Donovan to live out the elitist hippie lifestyle to which he has become accustomed.

BLOOD, SWEAT, AND TEARS
Blood, Sweat, and Tears
Columbia, 1969
highest chart position: number one (seven weeks)

Over the years, Al Kooper has gained a reputation as an ace session player (You know the organ on "Like a Rolling Stone?"—him), top producer (the first few Lynyrd Skynyrd albums), and hit songwriter ("This Diamond Ring" by one of Jerry's kids and the Playboys). In 1967, Kooper formed Blood, Sweat, and Tears as an attempt to (re)introduce elements of jazz and blues into rock without using the word "fusion."

Child Is Father to the Man, the group's first album, was a critical success, serving up versions of songs by such fine writers as Randy Newman, Tim Buckley, and Gerry Goffin and Carole King in a new setting, as well as a killer Kooper original, "I Can't Quit Her." Kooper, ever antsy to move on, then left the group to work with Mike Bloomfield and Stephen Stills on his *Super Session* records, as well as additional production chores. Too bad the rest of group wasn't so ambitious.

Blood, Sweat, and Tears's eponymous (rock critics have to use this word at least once in a book; by the way, we always use it wrong because the correct word is *homonymous*—take that, *Rolling Stone!*) second album was the first blast across the bow of rock and roll by the middle-of-the-road sound truck that ran over the hit radio and record charts of 1970. Blood, Sweat, and Tears hit upon the perfect formula. They watered down Kooper's original concept until rock was all but eroded and aimed its fuzzy concept of jazz and blues to a mass audience who never listened to or cared for either. In doing so, Blood, Sweat, and Tears instantly became one of the most popular groups of the early seventies.

Blood, Sweat, and Tears was a sampler record for the coming decade and as such should have been encouragement to would-be Rip Van Winkles. The seventies are here in all their horror. You get the pretentiousness; a song title like "Variations on a Theme by Erik Satie (First and Second Movements)" should suggest that there are no sly pop charms in it worth scouring for. You get long, boring instrumentals like "Blues—Part II," which rips off the lead line from Cream's "Sunshine of Your Love." You even get desecration of revered songs (Linda Ronstadt must have taken notes); this version of "God Bless the

Child" not only strips the song of its subtlety and therefore its power (no surprise there), but compounds the sin by breaking into a nonsensical Latin beat halfway through.

Oh yeah, the record was a big hit. *Blood, Sweat, and Tears* spent seven weeks at the top of the charts and vomited three number-two singles ("You've Made Me So Very Happy," "Spinning Wheel," "And When I Die"). Although Blood, Sweat, and Tears soon ran out of all three, their bad influence remained. Producer James William Guercio parlayed his success with them into a gig as producer for a like-minded group who gave nonjazzy arrangements to nonrock songs and, in the process, became an even bigger success than Blood, Sweat, and Tears: Chicago.

BRUCE WILLIS
The Return of Bruno
Motown, 1987
highest chart position: number fourteen

Bruce Willis doesn't play harmonica any worse than, say, Danny Partridge played bass, which is the best recommendation we can give to *The Return of Bruno*, the wretched vanity production that masqueraded as Willis's debut album. The problem on it was quite simple: Willis couldn't sing. This *other* New Jersey Bruce may have been a riot during the first season of "Moonlighting," but he had less than zero presence as a vocalist. A host of backup singers and arrangements busier than Willis's accountants barely managed to prop up these songs. One could say they died easily.

It's a measure of how powerless Willis was as a singer that he couldn't break through the record's unending soul clichés. The opening "Comin' Right Up" was a particularly blatant James Brown cop (more followed), featuring hackneyed horns that masked the tiny amount of wit in Willis's lecherous asides. "Jackpot (Bruno's Bop)," the only cut Willis bothered to cowrite, was a Louis Jordan–style jump-blues evocation as unpropulsive as a fuelless gas guzzler headed uphill.

Monumental incompetence aside, what made *The Return of Bruno* such an ample target for disgust was its gratuitously disrespectful attitude toward its classic cover choices. Unlike the Blues Brothers— another useless act, but at least they sounded somewhat interested in the culture they were exploiting—Willis did not sound as if he was reviving heartfelt favorites he had either grown up with or grown to love. Instead, he lazily used familiar tunes, like the Coasters' "Young Blood," the Drifters' "Under the Boardwalk," the Staple Singers' "Respect Yourself," and Johnny Rivers's "Secret Agent Man," as empty signifiers, cynical ploys to exploit the feel-good sound of the *Big Chill* generation, without hinting that he understood what the songs might mean. (This was Motown's idea of a soul revival?) He sang the lovely "Under the Boardwalk" in the same smug wine-cooler-commercial manner with which he defiled his uptempo selections. It sounded like Willis and coproducer Robert Kraft figured they didn't even need to make a record: all they needed to do was put Willis's smirk on a cover and it would sell. These spiritual children of P. T. Barnum were right.

Willis can be a genuinely funny and enjoyable performer: he can be likable as long as he does not open his mouth to sing. To place it where it belongs, *The Return of Bruno* is better than any album by Telly Savalas, Sebastian Cabot, or Leonard Nimoy, but compare it with a real record and it crumbles like a bad sitcom.

STARSHIP
Knee Deep in the Hoopla
Grunt, 1985
highest chart position: number seventeen

Somewhere along the line, rock bands started to bear an uneasy resemblance to sports teams. It doesn't matter who you are; as long as you wear the same shirt as everybody standing around you, you're part of the group.

In 1965, Paul Kantner founded a rock band called Jefferson Airplane. During the Summer of Love, the Airplane and the Grateful Dead were the bands of choice among San Francisco's flower children too stoned to opt for Creedence Clearwater Revival. During the late sixties and early seventies, the group went through numerous personnel changes, finally hitting a consistent platinum stride as Jefferson Starship. By 1985, however, all the original members of the band, including Kantner, had disappeared; only the replacements remained (Grace Slick was not an original member). Although they still wanted to record under the Jefferson Starship moniker, Kantner owned the legal rights to at least the "Jefferson" part of the name, so the band was reduced to Starship. Seem like a fair deal to you? Everybody always called the band "Starship" anyway and Kantner got to keep the, er, historical part of the name. Everybody made out except for the folks who got stuck knee-deep when they bought this crap.

Knee Deep in the Hoopla kicks off with the would-be anthem "We Built This City." Presumably a paean to their hometown San Francisco, "We Built This City" contains enough self-congratulation that even if it weren't as musically atrocious and lyrically confusing as it is, it would still qualify as one of the most annoying songs ever recorded. Dragged along by a shriek of synthesizers and electronic drums, the song comes off as if it weren't composed so much as randomly programmed—right down to the invocation of rock and roll as the bedrock of society. Of course the egotistical implication here is that this band—or, more appropriately, one of its full-named forebears—was responsible in no small part for the image of San Fran as a rock-and-roll city. Now that's what we call feeling good about yourself.

In "We Built This City," the best insult they can come up with is Slick's lines, "Someone's always playing/Corporation games/Who cares? They're always changing/Corporation names." Does that remind you of any band Grace? The song later took on special ironic significance when it turned up on the soundtrack for an ITT television commercial. So much for sticking it to corporate stooges.

The synthesizers heard throughout the album, provided by producer Peter Wolf (not Faye Dunaway's ex), do what synthesizers seem to do in the hands of minor talents: they mask the fact that there's no song in the immediate vicinity. Behind the bouncy riff of "Hearts of the World (Will Understand)," for instance, are such lyrics as "My mind is torn between right and wrong/The two extremes and I hate it./I won't give in to you just because you want me to./Ooh, life's so complicated." Isn't it?

This isn't the only service that producer Wolf provided for the band: he also showed them how to pad out an album by dragging out an ending so that it's almost as long as the song itself ("Love Rusts") or by giving a seemingly already completed track a false ending and tagging on another ending. Too bad he didn't just tell them that they needed another song, but then again he probably thought he was doing the listeners a favor.

After a couple of albums with this Starship, Slick finally learned the rules of follow-the-leader and left the group, this time to re-form with the late-sixties version of the Jefferson Airplane for a reunion album under that name. (It stiffed.) We understand that they're going to take some time off and get back together to celebrate the twenty-fifth anniversary of the Summer of Love. Only they're going to change their name again. This time they'll be the Jefferson Wheelchair.

THE BEACH BOYS
Still Cruisin'
Capitol, 1989
highest chart position: number ninety-three

For those waiting for the Beach Boys to hit rock bottom, the suspense ended with the release of this record. After a brief artistic comeback in the mid-seventies (on record, anyway), the formerly worthwhile group jettisoned any remaining idea of doing something new or remotely controversial (unless you count the James Watt mess or Mike Love's PMRC support) and chose instead to coast on past glories. Every summer the Beach Boys tour the same halls and offer perfunctory performances of their most obvious hits; every summer they sound more tired and musically bankrupt. We saw the Beach Boys at Roosevelt Stadium in Jersey City in 1976 and thought they were washed up; this album was recorded a dozen years later. Now they only play stadiums between baseball games and fireworks exhibitions.

Still Cruisin' paired seven recent recordings (four of which had already been released) with three unassailable Beach Boys classics from the sixties, which were included in this set under the dubious proposition that they had been heard in recent films. It was doubtful, however, that anyone listened to "California Girls" and relived memories of *Soul Man.* The three oldies padded the record to a point at which it was nearly listenable. The arid, tropical "Kokomo," which became a freak hit after it was included in *Cocktail* (a Tom Cruise vehicle nearly as hateful as the racist *Soul Man),* set the pattern for the new, passion-free songs. "Kokomo" works if your idea of a good Beach Boys song is one that rhymes *Bermuda, Jamaica,* and *take ya.* Otherwise go back to "Surfin' U.S.A."; at least most of us can afford to go to the sites listed in that song. Not to be curmudgeons, but we've always noticed that, as wonderful as the Beach Boys' early records were, there was always an element of elitism in them—if you didn't drive the right make of car, ride the right brand of boogie board, hang out with the right group of guys, or date the girl with the blondest hair, you couldn't be in the club—but by "Kokomo" that mere adolescent cliquishness had been subsumed by cranky, middle-aged arrogance.

The nadir of *Still Cruisin'* was its title track, a cynical rewrite of "Kokomo," proving that the middle-aged Beach Boys will do anything for a hit. Don't they make enough money flogging their old hits to television advertising agencies? Brian Wilson's sole new contribution, "In My Car," was slight, but it was the only one of the newies that didn't hurt much if you listened to it more than once. *Still Cruisin'* was stillborn.

IRON BUTTERFLY
Live

Atco, 1970

highest chart position: number twenty

You want bombast? It doesn't get any more bombastic than this.

In the late sixties, when Atlantic Records founder-genius Ahmet Ertegun ascertained that he wasn't going to be able to cut hits with Aretha Franklin or Otis Redding (or any of the other star soul marvels) forever, he looked to broaden his base. The ascent of the Yardbirds indicated to forward-leaning ears that the commercial future was going to be in heavy rock. Ertegun promptly snatched a promising British band called Led Zeppelin, who didn't have much trouble earning out their advance. Ertegun also signed an American group of bloozebusters called Iron Butterfly.

The San Diego quintet's first album bombed, but on their follow-up they exceeded everyone's sales expectations; for a short time it was the largest-selling album in Atlantic history. The second side of *In-a-Gadda-Da-Vida* offered only one song, a seventeen-minute version of the album title. Few "classic rock" songs plodded harder or longer than "In-a-Gadda-Da-Vida." In essence, the song is a facile mumbling of a silly nursery rhyme (In-a-Gadda-Da-Vida, In-the-garden-of-Eden, get it?) played over and over and over and over and over. The drum solo alone in "In-a-Gadda-Da-Vida" was nearly three minutes long, longer than nearly every single released by Sun Records in its heyday.

"In-a-Gadda-Da-Vida" and most of Iron Butterfly's other recordings were a series of solos. This method made sense because none of the band members seemed willing to play together. By the time they released their fourth LP, *Live*, two years after their debut (strike while the iron's hot), only three members, including keyboardist, singer, and main songwriter Doug Ingle, remained from the original five-piece. Everybody played their own parts with verve and then slipped into automatic pilot when it was someone else's turn. On some songs, among them "In-a-Gadda-Da-Vida," band members would simply leave the stage during other members' solos. They weren't involved enough to hang around.

Live is the apotheosis of blooze excess. Its riffs are more wordy and distorted than those of Vanilla Fudge; Ingle's attempts at emotion-filled singing usually mean that he yells "Huh!" a bit louder and longer. Ensemble playing is nonexistent; throughout the album, organ, guitar, and vocal all fight for the same useless space. When one of them gets a chance alone in the spotlight, the arrangement gets even muddier. Ingle's sub–Keith Emerson organ shoves instruments aside like a dumb bully; each of his many Nice solos is nothing but another chance to play the main riff from the *Nutcracker*'s "March of the Wooden Soldiers" ad nauseam.

Speaking of nausea, the inevitable side-length version of "In-a-Gadda-Da-Vida" included here clocks in at nineteen minutes and change, more than two minutes longer than the interminable studio version. (This is like finding a new brand of aspirin that makes the pain last longer.) Any hopes that the two extra minutes would be used to explain what the damn thing was all about were quashed immediately. All you get are longer solos. It sounds like the guitarist bought his first wah-wah pedal just before the show and can't stop playing with it; he certainly isn't playing it. More than once a false ending appears. You think the song is over, you feel the sound levels begin to fade out, but no: organ solo! drum solo! another organ solo! All this garbage on an Atlantic record: at least Otis wasn't around to hear it.

BON JOVI
Slippery When Wet
Mercury, 1986
highest chart position: number one (eight weeks)

How many clichés can you squeeze into a single pop song? Probably not as many as Jon Bon Jovi can.

For proof, listen to "Raise Your Hands" from his mammoth album *Slippery When Wet*. (We know, that's two already, but titles don't count.) In the song, the former Jon Bongiovi lets loose with "nasty reputation," "sticky situation," "ain't nobody better," "show me what you can do," "under the gun," "out on the run," "set the night on fire," "playin' to win."

Impressive, no? And that's only the first verse.

Perhaps we're being unfair. Nobody listens to Bon Jovi's brand of pop for its lyrics; they listen because they want to bang their heads lightly. It's a style of music played by half the bands on MTV. A grafting of hard-rock style onto safe-as-milk teenybopper fluff, it's a genre that has come to be known as power ballads or bubblemetal. A canny marketing strategy (no doubt dreamed up by their convicted drug-dealer manager, Doc McGhee), the sound almost doesn't work for Bon Jovi because the band members are barely functional. The guitar solos (by Richie Sambora, one of Cher's more recent minor pop-star conquests) sound like afterthoughts, the bass lines whine like spoiled children, and Jon Bon Jovi's voice is frequently double- and triple-tracked in halfhearted attempts to cloak its fundamental blandness. Bon Jovi stumbles into sentimental territory on "Never Say Goodbye," but delicacy is not this band's strong suit; Meat Loaf is subtle compared to these guys. The callous clinker "Remember when we lost the keys/And you lost more than that in my back seat" is Meat Head Jovi's idea of evocative storytelling.

Which makes it bizarre that the three megahit singles from *Slippery When Wet* were taken to reflect Jon's newfound ability to be a spokesman for a generation of young, working-class kids. Maybe since Bruce Springsteen was ensconced in one of his epic studio hibernations when *Slippery When Wet* came out, and the rock audience figured they had to get some salt-of-the-earth wisdom from a New Jersey guitarist, Jon got the post by default. For whatever reason, Jon became a legit star. Yet even the most cursory listen to his three smash singles—"You Give Love a Bad Name," "Livin' on a Prayer," and

"Wanted Dead or Alive"—gives the lie to such respectability. "You Give Love a Bad Name" is pop metal at its most whiny; every edge is sanded down. "Livin' on a Prayer" tries to be an anthem for kids in trouble, but its lyrics cut it down at the roots: if "it doesn't really matter if we make it or not," why does the narrator suggest they try? And then why does he sing, "Take my hand/We'll make it, I swear?" (Forget for a moment that we never get a concrete clue as to what they're trying to do.)

"Wanted Dead or Alive" is the funniest; think of it as Ennio Morricone meets Pee-Wee Herman in a cowboy suit. Its linking of six-guns and six-strings is a direct steal from Billy Joel's equally failed self-mythology, "The Legend of Billy the Kid," and its affected, Wild West sound makes the posturing even more ludicrous (*you* try to sit straight-faced through lines like "I've seen a million faces/And I've rocked them all"). No wonder this song convinced the producers of *Young Guns II*, another work about the West with the credibility of a "Hee Haw" sketch, that Bon was the right man to score the film. Jon responded with eight permutations of "Wanted Dead or Alive," some of which had the same chord changes.

Jon Bon Jovi and his band made millions (before Jon temporarily broke up the group in 1989—for artistic reasons, if you can believe it) serving up condescending sentiment and reducing every emotion to a bare-faced cliché—either because they thought that's all their audience could comprehend or because that's all *they* could comprehend. On *Slippery When Wet*, their worst and most popular album, Bon Jovi sounds like bad fourth-generation soft metal, a smudgy Xerox of Quiet Riot, Pat Boone in leather.

ROLLING STONES
Still Life (American Concert 1981)
Rolling Stones, 1982
highest chart position: number five

Hey! Live records are supposed to convey the excitement and intensity of a concert performance. This idea also filters down to the titles of live albums, which frequently have exclamation points in them, like Ted Nugent's *Double Live Gonzo!*, Tom Petty and the Heartbreakers' *Pack Up the Plantation—Live!*, and the Stones' own *Got Live If You Want It!* and *"Get Yer Ya-Ya's Out!"* Even with some dubious live sets (Mary Kay Place's *Tonight! At the Capri Lounge—Loretta Haggers)*, some folks feel that a dynamic live title will grab attention. That said, the Rolling Stones' *Still Life* is a perfectly descriptive title for a live album that is as energetic as a plastic-fruit centerpiece.

Still Life documented the formerly Greatest Rock-and-Roll Band in the World's tour in support of their *Tattoo You* LP. (The Jovan-sponsored journey also yielded a Hal Ashby nonfilm, *Let's Spend the Night Together*, which, naturally, smelled.) Unlike *Love You Live* (1976), a double live set the Stones recorded during one of their periodic creative stupors (much like guitarist Keith Richards's heroin-induced lethargy of the time), this single-LP set should have been wonderful. *Tattoo You* (1981) was a spirited record propelled by future album-radio standards "Start Me Up" and "Waiting on a Friend." Simply, it was an encouraging return to unencumbered form after 1980's *Emotional Rescue,* a blatant retread of *Some Girls* (1978) that consisted primarily of compositions wisely left off the previous record. And a brief perusal of the album's song list was encouraging. Except for "(I Can't Get No) Satisfaction," which had sounded lame and pro forma onstage for years, and Eddie Cochran's "Twenty Flight Rock," a rockabilly strut that showcased none of this R&B-leaning group's strengths, the remaining eight tracks seemed ideal, a canny mix of old ("Under My Thumb"), new ("Shattered," "Start Me Up"), and a pair of Motown covers idiosyncratic enough to rise above pronto–*Big Chill* nostalgia (Smokey Robinson's "Going to a Go-Go" and the Temptations' "Just My Imagination").

Expectations are lowered several thousand feet within seconds after the Stones begin playing. Unlike previous Stones live sets that begin with boasting announcers ("Ladies and gentlemen: The greatest rock-and-roll band in the world!"), this one limps out of the gate with an apologetic "Thank you very, very much for waiting, New Jersey." The band starts playing the familiar opening to "Under My Thumb," but you immediately realize that something is off. The tempo drags a bit, and the intro goes on far too long. Where's Mick? Slapping hands with fans at the lip of the stage? Undergoing a last-minute wardrobe change? Confirming reservations at Elaine's for after the show? Keeping Bianca's lawyers away from the gate receipts? Whatever Jagger is doing, his delayed entrance starts the show on the wrong thumb. His singing stresses the wrong syllables, and that encourages guitarists Richards and Ron Wood to do what they do worst, solo to fill spaces. "Take it easy," Jagger moans, and he follows his own advice. Still, drummer Charlie Watts pushes everyone else along efficiently enough to see to it that this "Under My Thumb" is not so much appalling as just a decidedly unexciting opener.

Speaking of appalling, no drummer can cover for an overwhelming performer like Jagger, who can't think of anything better at song's end to say than, "Hey, welcome Virginia. [Wait a second: weren't we just in New Jersey?] Welcome Hampton. Welcome to everyone watchin' on TV. Hope you're havin' a good time there, drinkin' a few beers, smokin' a few joints, all right." In the next song, "Let's Spend the Night Together," the evening begins to unravel. Uninformed guitars push keyboards (played by the implacable, glimmering Ian twins, Stewart and MacLagan) into the corner of the mix, and Keith's hoarse harmonies are desperate cries for Robitussin (if not something stronger). *Still Life* collapses completely on the third song, "Shattered." Ten minutes into the record (by now they're in Phoenix or Honolulu or somewhere), Mick has stopped working, rushing "Shattered" so nonsensically it's easy to wonder if he just wants to get the gig over with so he can go to the after-show party backstage. Poor, uninvolved Mick is so stuck on autopilot that he can't stop resorting to "Are you ready to rock and roll, [your city here]?" babbles that make him sound like a heavy-metal support group singer.

As if the shtick isn't bad enough, there's also the music. The most telling (read: most depressing) song here is "Time Is on My Side," which sounds tired, distracted, affected (dig Mick's Southern accent), and unintentionally ironic, a sluggish slumber. If time is on their side, bet against time. They played this song every night of the tour and must have recorded all their shows: this was the best version they could come up with?

Oh yeah, we ought to tell you about the squalid movie *Let's Spend the Night Together,* drawn like blood (sorry, Keith) from the same desiccated performances. Perhaps what's most welcome about *Still Life,* aside from the fact that it's not a double record, is that you don't have to look at Mick. (Keith looks as he always does—as if he is about to die.) When he's not running laps, our hero, garbed in a football jersey and skintight yellow pants, drags us through the same moves— Jerry Lewis meets Marcel Marceau in a Parisian strip joint—that have made him a laughingstock since 1975.

The Rolling Stones eventually righted themselves. In the latter half of the eighties, they came up with two worthy records, *Dirty Work* and the overrated-but-still-good *Steel Wheels.* But after the three-headed disaster (tour, record, film) of 1981–82, it seemed for a while as though the greatest ensemble players in rock and roll no longer had anything to say to each other.

MCAD2-8018

THE WHO
Who's Last
MCA, 1984

highest chart position: number eighty-one

The Who have released more compilation albums and live albums than records of new material. Since 1965, the band has put out ten studio sets; in that same period there have been twelve official releases of live recordings, rarities, soundtracks featuring material already available in one form or another, greatest-hits collections, and otherwise unreleased material. And don't forget the film soundtracks or the all-star orchestral versions of *Tommy* or Pete Townshend's two *Scoop* collections of Who demos.

Two of those live albums (*Who's Last, Join Together*) come from tours that took place after the Who stopped being a working band. In 1983 the band decided to break up. To celebrate this announcement (which most fans felt should have been made in 1978 after Keith Moon died), the band embarked on what was promised to be their last tour. *Who's Last* documents the final show from what must now be considered their first farewell tour. We just happen to know it was the last show; the information wasn't in the factually vacuous packaging. Perhaps the band members knew the record was a stinker and didn't want any of their names on it.

Who's Last is a sad statement. Throughout four sides (or two CDs that total less than seventy-six minutes) the band performs rote versions of the same songs they've been serving up for years. You almost can't blame Roger Daltrey for sounding so tired on this record: he must be as sick of singing these songs as we are of hearing them. *You* try to go out there and sing "See Me, Feel Me" for the 4,686th time.

That probably also explains why the entire band sounds as focused as the Hubble Telescope. Townshend replays stale licks, and although Kenney Jones was not a disastrous replacement for Keith Moon, warhorses like "Baba O'Riley" suffer from the lack of Moon's full-frontal assaults.

And then there's "Long Live Rock." This alleged rock anthem was never one of the Who's greatest songs to begin with. It was probably never even one of the band's personal favorites, since it only saw the light of day on the outtakes collection *Odds and Sods* in 1974 and didn't become a radio standard until it appeared on the soundtrack *The Kids Are Alright* in 1979. (See what we mean about rehashing material?) On *Who's Last*, "Long Live Rock" is rushed through in a manner even it doesn't deserve, but just when you think the song is mercifully over, it's back with a "Reprise" wherein Townshend tries to turn it into a honky-tonk boogie. As it turns out, listening to Pete try to sing like Moon Mullican is the funniest thing since Daltrey tried to get his vocal chords around the Gilbert and Sullivan *hommage* "Helpless Dancer" on *Quadrophenia*.

The only song on the set that Who fans didn't already have in at least one previous, superior version is the cover of the Beatles' cover of the Isley Brothers' "Twist and Shout." Like Eddie Cochran's "Summertime Blues" (also included on *Who's Last*, in a vastly inferior version to that on *Live at Leeds*), "Twist and Shout" is one of those elemental rockers that you can't do a bad version of unless you try extremely hard. The only reason it survives on *Who's Last* is that the Who weren't capable of trying extremely hard.

VAN DYKE PARKS
Song Cycle
Warner Brothers, 1968
highest chart position: did not chart

When fans and critics label the Beach
Boys' Brian Wilson a genius, they frequently invoke his work on *Smile*,
an album that was never released because Brian went crazy. This is like
getting full credit for a school project that you never handed in just
because you were a pretty good student beforehand. *Smile* is wrapped
in such mystique nowadays that not only has it been proclaimed the
Beach Boys' greatest triumph by people who have never heard it, but
Van Dyke Parks, Wilson's songwriting partner on the album, was also
automatically hailed as a genius even though nobody had ever heard
anything by him.

Parks's debut album, *Song Cycle*, released a year after *Smile* wasn't,
was immediately proclaimed one of the greatest records ever released,
again by a cabal many of whom hadn't heard it. Allegedly pieced
together over four years, *Song Cycle*'s twelve overorchestrated tracks
are rampant with bad rhymes sung in a fey voice designed to make you
say, "Oh, gosh, what a genius." Instead, you lose interest after the first
two minutes. Just because you've been told something is a masterpiece
doesn't mean it is. If you disagree, we have a truckload of Byrds
reunion cassettes we've been trying to dump. Use your brain.

That's the last thing Parks wants his listeners to do. *Song Cycle* is a
record conceived for a cult audience. Like religious cults, rock cults are
all about idolizing a fundamentally flawed performer and applauding
his every wrong move: when Robyn Hitchcock called one of his records
Queen Elvis, the only people who didn't get the joke were him and his
audience. Cult audiences value cleverness over direct expression and
the abstract over clarity. Keep doing what you're doing, they say to
their leader; our allegiance just proves how much cooler we are than
everyone else. The whole insular point of *Song Cycle* is to prove the
performer's cleverness, and by extension the sagacity of those chosen
few along for the ride.

Parks's wan, affected voice shows the artist's hand immediately. Parks
is a Southerner (born in Mississippi or Alabama, depending on which
press release you believe), but he wants to sound like an erudite
Northeastern fop, pretentious beyond his years. This voice babbles bad
rhymes, like "She made perfume in the back of the room," and verbose
say-whatever-comes-to-mind lines, like "He is not your run-of-the-

mill, garden-variety, Alabama country fair," not to mention enough knee-jerk antitechnology dogma to make you want to send money to Raytheon. His precious warble starts each song looking for a melody but soon gives up and revels in its own insularity.

Don't let this bother you: you're never going to get to the lyrics, because the music that cloaks them is so frustratingly dense. On *Song Cycle*, Parks gives you orchestrations instead of arrangements. Instead of thinking out the songs and figuring out what best serves them, like arrangers are supposed to do, Parks throws in everything he can find—from tuba to bird noises (on "Palm Desert")—and hopes it adds up to something. Cuteness runs rampant. Two brief, pointless nonevocations bear the same name, "Laurel Canyon Blvd," and a song called "Van Dyke Parks," credited to Public Domain, is followed by "Public Domain," credited to, you guessed it, Van Dyke Parks. Nobody could replicate the all-over-the-place sound of this record, but many nascent performers picked up on Parks's vague-and-verbose-as-possible attitude. These kids became the art rockers that clutter sports arenas to this day, foisting self-aggrandizing sub–Ayn Randian ideas on fourteen-year-olds from coast to coast.

Parks subsequently did come up with some fine work. His *Discover America* (1972) was a witty, tour de force journey throughout a variety of Caribbean rhythms, and his string arranging for Sam Phillips (the pop singer, not the Sun Records icon) made his orchestral dreams come true. But it's *Song Cycle* that Parks and his legions point to as evidence of the auteur's genius. *Song Cycle* is a classic precisely because most rock fans have never heard it. Those unfortunate enough to find it out will be terribly disappointed.

Kind of like *Smile*.

ROGER WATERS
Radio K.A.O.S.
Columbia, 1987
highest chart position: number fifty

Every few years a special kind of album emerges. An album fueled by colossal ineptitude and a perversely fascinating inability to communicate even the simplest idea without wrapping it in pretension. *Radio K.A.O.S.*, Roger Waters's second concept album since leaving Pink Floyd to make mountains of money without him, was such an album.

Waters's first Floyd-free record, *The Pros and Cons of Hitchhiking*, was also a mess, a confused, self-pitying tale of how hard it is to be a rock star. (All those high-paying jobs, all that leisure time, all those fringe benefits. What travails! Why would anyone stoop to live such a horrible life? Could it be the promise of enormous fame and money? Naah.) It did, however, have Eric Clapton guesting on guitar throughout, which made for the occasional listenable moment. *Radio K.A.O.S.* didn't even have that much going for it. The only guest star of any consequence on *Radio K.A.O.S.* was occasional singer and keyboard player Paul Carrack, whose part in Mike + the Mechanics' "The Living Years" you already know about.

Radio K.A.O.S. is the story of Benny, a Welsh coal miner who loves his ham radio, and his twin brother, Billy, who is a vegetable. For reasons too complicated and random to encapsulate, Billy disembowels telephones for kicks and Benny gets shipped off to America. Their great-uncle David feels guilty because he invented the atom bomb. Benny befriends an obnoxious Los Angeles disc jockey, Billy saves the world from nuclear destruction, and Uncle Dave starts to feel a little better about himself after seeing Live Aid on the telly. The album ends.

We are relating the story because there is no music to write about. In Pink Floyd's later albums, Waters's relatively straightforward individual tunes helped carry his convoluted storylines. But *Radio K.A.O.S.* offered sound effects instead of arrangements and jarring increases in volume to cloak an inability to convey either emotions or melodies. (Warning: If an album starts with a noise instead of a voice or instrument, the safest course of action is to return it to the store and say it was defective. You won't be lying.) Individual songs were incomprehensible without the lengthy libretto (which, alas, was enclosed), and the lyrics are heavy-handed ("How do you make a have out of a have-not?"), muddled ("They like fear and loathing/They like sheep's clothing"), or received ("Forgive me, Father, for I have sinned. It was either me or him").

Worst of all was Waters's voice, so burned out from years of screaming you could almost smell the ashes. *Radio K.A.O.S.* was what happened when an aging pop performer deluded himself into thinking that his ideas were so grand they transcended pop-song form. The only problem here is that there weren't enough trenchant ideas to fill a song, let alone a whole album.

Needless to say, both the album *Radio K.A.O.S.* and the tour supporting it were enormous critical and commercial bombs. Waters's elaborate tour started out playing in two-thirds-empty arenas and ended up shifting to small, half-filled theaters. The slight must have hurt Waters all the more because, at the same time, his ex-bandmates in Pink Floyd were going double platinum with their own lame album, *A Momentary Lapse of Reason,* and touring to overflowing arenas and stadiums, setting several ticket-sales records along the way. Unfazed, Waters went into the seclusion of his recording studio and, through his publicist, announced his next project: *Radio K.A.O.S., Part II.* We can't wait: perhaps this volume will have songs on it.

Part II hasn't shown up yet, but since *Radio K.A.O.S.* came out, Waters kicked the carcass of Pink Floyd one more time, performing "The Wall" at the Berlin Wall. East and West are uniting, but Waters and David Gilmour refuse to make up.

BOB DYLAN
Live at Budokan
Columbia, 1978
highest chart position: number thirteen

Nineteen seventy-eight was a year of comebacks for sixties vets. The Rolling Stones roared back to life with *Some Girls;* the Kinks yielded the surprisingly down-to-earth *Misfits;* and the Who scored with *Who Are You,* their fiercest set in years. Bob Dylan went to Japan and made the most preposterous live album by a major performer in the history of rock and roll.

Dylan spent the first half of the seventies building up speed after his downfall. He finally regained his stride in a 1974 tour with the Band and subsequent albums *Blood on the Tracks* and *Desire.* Dylan's stock gradually fell after that, accompanied by personal and artistic desperation. In 1978, he hit rock bottom. His marriage fell apart, his surrealistic, four-hour-plus travelogue film *Renaldo and Clara* was released to widespread confusion followed by indifference, his LP *Street Legal* was even more impenetrable, and he seemed to be toying with a new belief system each week. If ever a record shows a man at the end of his rope with no redemption available or conceivable, *Live at Budokan* is it.

By 1978 Dylan had made much of his career by confounding expectations. His previous seventies live albums (among top-rank performers, only Elvis Presley put out more) featured drastically reconstructed versions of his chestnuts, but at least on *The Concert for Bangladesh, Before the Flood,* and *Hard Rain* (not to mention the aborted soundtrack to *Renaldo and Clara),* Dylan sounded involved in his songs and stubbornly sought to find new meanings in them, both for himself and his audience. On *Live at Budokan,* he played drastically reconstructed versions of his chestnuts because he was bored with them. The arrangements are random, indiscriminate ("Don't Think Twice, It's All Right" as reggae, for instance), and stupefying. It's like a game of "Name That Tune": can you guess the song before Dylan gets to the chorus?

Maybe Bob was so sick of his songs and his reputation that he just wanted to throw it all away and start from scratch. Maybe Bob was jealous of Cheap Trick, whose own *At Budokan* was their commercial breakthrough. Maybe Bob wanted to work out the kinks in his prospective Las Vegas act. Maybe Bob thought a quickie live album would recoup his considerable *Renaldo and Clara* debts. Maybe Bob

was so mad at saxophonist Steve Douglas that he wanted to embarrass the squawker before the widest possible audience. Maybe Bob thought his original records weren't available in Japan and no one would know the difference. Maybe Bob lost a bet with a Tokyo promoter.

We could make such conjectures all day (and we would if our editor would uncock his .38), but even a garbage dump full of A. J. Webermans couldn't explain away the hatred that absorbs Dylan on *Live at Budokan.* By this, we don't mean the sort of cranky, petulant nihilism that Lou Reed pointed at critics on *Take No Prisoners;* this is full-blown misanthropy directed at his audience (they'll clap at anything), his songs (they won't die no matter how hard he tries to kill them), and himself (I don't want to be Bob Dylan anymore). How better to abandon one's following, one's song catalogue, and oneself than by an act of unforgivable callousness?

Live at Budokan asks, "What does Bob Dylan care about?" Certainly not these twenty-one tunes, most of them among his most lasting in earlier incarnations. Fifteen years of playing "Blowin' in the Wind" could drive any performer mad, and only madness can explain why Dylan would turn the timeless tale into a puffy melodrama geared for casino theaters. His ascending vocal in the final chorus is a Borscht Belt affectation as worn out as a seventies lounge singer's lime-green leisure suit. When outraged fans label *Live at Budokan* a Vegas move, they're not exaggerating: they're describing a show that "climaxes" with Dylan and band returning for an encore of "The Times They Are A-Changin'," which the former rebel introduces with all the fake sincerity of the late Sammy Davis, Jr., crooning "Candy Man." Dylan says, "Thank you. You're so very kind. You really are. We'll play you this song. I wrote this about fifteen years ago. It still means a lot to me. I know it means a lot to you too." This from a man who once said, "If I told you what my music was about, we'd all be arrested." Unfortunately, complacency is not a criminal offense.

Speaking of criminals, everyone in Dylan's eleven-piece band deserves to do hard time for nonsupport, but special attention should be directed at Steve Douglas. On saxophone, flute, and recorder, Douglas manages to suck the life out of all he plays. His high-end squeals on "Mr. Tambourine Man" and "All Along the Watchtower" break the already brittle recastings; when he finally does his Clarence Clemons impersonation in "Forever Young," you wish the Big Man would sit on the little creep and sew his lips together.

As is to be expected of such miss-and-miss arrangements, one wild one occasionally works, like the mind-boggling, hard-rock recasting of "It's Allright Ma (I'm Only Bleeding)." It's an accident, proving that even at his worst Dylan is worth hearing. As Dylan has learned throughout his career (trying to shed folkies, rockers, Joan Baez, and most recently his evangelical Christian pals), he can't disappear. As with *Self Portrait* and his most rigid religious work, overzealous and underthinking fans have championed *Live at Budokan* as the most harmful action a major American has inflicted on the Japanese people since Harry Truman gave the go-ahead to level Nagasaki (or at least since Sidney Sheldon translations appeared on their shores).

VARIOUS PERFORMERS
70's Hits: Great Records of the Decade—
The Original Recordings, Volume 1
Curb, 1990
highest chart position: yeah, right
(Although, if you figure it out, these ten songs
spent a total of 201 weeks on the charts.)

No rock decade has seen the release and chart success of more lousy songs than the seventies. We're willing to bet that if you named your own personal list of worst rock songs, three-quarters of them would be from the seventies. Looking back, you can summarize the decade's chart action when you realize that "Raindrops Keep Falling on My Head" was the number-one song for the entire month of January 1970 and "Escape (The Piña Colada Song)" closed out the decade as the top song. In with a whimper, out with a whimper. In between you had Helen Reddy, Barry Manilow, Mac Davis, Tony Orlando and Dawn, the Captain and Tennille, Olivia Newton-John, and that's not even to mention bubble gum or disco. At times it seemed as if the pop charts had been confined to ten years of purgatory and the only person allowed in who could recognize a beat was Paul McCartney, and he kept singing "Silly Love Songs."

All of which plays havoc with record companies when they try to release compilation sets using the seventies as a theme. Some labels have deliberately turned the decade into a joke. Rhino Records has put out a fifteen-volume set of songs from the decade under the title *Have a Nice Day*, with the smiley face and everything. If Rhino had put out the set on limited-edition eight-track tapes, the joke would have been perfect.

What it took Rhino fifteen records to do, however, Curb managed to accomplish in a single mind-numbing set. And they weren't treating it as a joke. Their *70's Hits: Great Records of the Decade—The Original Recordings, Volume 1* stands as a primer of the worst hits from that ten-year period. Take a look at this lineup:
"You Light Up My Life" **by Debby Boone**
"Let Your Love Flow" **by the Bellamy Brothers**
"Kiss You All Over" **by Exile**
"December 1963 (Oh What a Night)" **by the Four Seasons**
"My Melody of Love" **by Bobby Vinton**
"That's Rock 'n' Roll" **by Shaun Cassidy**
"Daddy Don't You Walk So Fast" **by Wayne Newton**
"Burning Bridges" **by the Mike Curb Congregation**
"The Candy Man" **by Sammy Davis, Jr.**
"Different Worlds" **by Maureen McGovern**

70's HITS

GREAT RECORDS OF THE DECADE

VOLUME 1

The Original Recordings

YOU LIGHT UP MY LIFE..DEBBY BOONE
LET YOUR LOVE FLOW ....THE BELLAMY BROTHERS
KISS YOU ALL OVER...EXILE
DECEMBER 1963 (OH WHAT A NIGHT)....THE FOUR SEASONS
MY MELODY OF LOVE....................................BOBBY VINTON
THAT'S ROCK 'N' ROLL ....SHAUN CASSIDY
DADDY DON'T YOU WALK SO FAST ....WAYNE NEWTON
BURNING BRIDGES..................MIKE CURB CONGREGATION
THE CANDY MAN............................SAMMY DAVIS, JR.
DIFFERENT WORLDS............................MAUREEN McGOVERN

K-Tel couldn't have done a better job. For instance, "You Light Up My Life" is probably mentioned most often when people discuss terrible songs, which is only fitting since it was the top song of the decade, having spent ten weeks at the number-one slot (that's longer than DiMaggio's fifty-six-game hitting streak in 1941, although the record is as exciting as one of Joe's off days during that period). A textbook example of schmaltz from the "Without You I'm Nothing" school of songwriting, it has probably been played at more weddings than any other song except "New York, New York" and "Celebrate." Everything about this song seems designed to parody love songs: from the gentle piano opening and studied vocal presentation to the final rising crescendo of strings, woodwinds, and overemphatic declaration of never-ending love. The lyrics, written by producer Joe Brooks, indulge in the worst kind of cloying sentiment (you already know the words; we won't repeat them). The most lasting emotion you're left with by the end of "You Light Up My Life" is the overwhelming desire to punch someone's lights out.

At least they got the right person to sing "You Light Up My Life"; you could expect a song this bad from Pat Boone's daughter. But who ever thought Shaun Cassidy was the right person to sing a song called "That's Rock 'n' Roll"? Shaun had followed in half-brother David's steps by starring in a bad television show and turning it into a singing career. In this case the show was "The Hardy Boys Mysteries," where he and fellow heartthrob-to-the-prepubescent-set Parker Stevenson portrayed updated versions of teen detectives Joe and Frank Hardy, who, when not solving cases, pursued their careers as—yeah, big surprise—rock-and-roll singers. Cassidy had a number-one record with a remake of "Da Doo Ron Ron" that tried to be note-for-note and came close, although the original's thrill of discovery fell off when he painted by numbers. Cassidy followed it up with his version of Eric ("All by myself/I wrote this song all by myself") Carmen's "That's Rock 'n' Roll." Even at his least grating, Carmen was definitely coming from the poppiest side of rock in the first place, but having Shaun Cassidy cover one of his songs is like having Christopher Guest write a comedy sketch for Alan Thicke: no matter how good it might be, it's going to come down to the level of the performer.

(Pointless aside we can't fit anywhere else: In 1989 we heard a radio interview with Shaun in which he complained that his producers took him away from the "raw rock and roll" he had been performing "in the club." That's right, folks: Shaun Cassidy would have invented punk rock if he had been allowed to. We now return to our entry, still in progress.)

"You Light Up My Life" and "That's Rock 'n' Roll" are bookends, the extremes of *70's Hits: Great Records of the Decade—The Original Recordings, Volume 1.* The record ranges from awful schlock pop to awful pop schlock. If you want to relive memories of Bobby Vinton's Polish joke, "My Melody of Love," or Wayne Newton's road to nowhere, "Daddy Don't You Walk So Fast," you need this record.

If you do need this record, however, we recommend stealing it, because much of the revenue from it goes to Mike Curb. Curb, reactionary California politician and even more reactionary record executive, has made a career of embarrassing himself by linking his antirock world view with his inability to pay the mortgage without rock. He's the closest thing to Mitch Miller we have nowadays. Curb is the kind of industry mogul who thinks it's a good idea to have a choral group (the Mike Curb Congregation, who make the Mormon Tabernacle Choir sound like the Soul Stirrers) cover the John Fogerty songbook. If you want to support that, go ahead. But we'd rather you give the money to Rhino.

THE MOODY BLUES
Days of Future Passed

Dream, 1967

highest chart position: number three

In the late sixties a new phenomenon over-
whelmed rock and roll. Upon the release of the Beatles' *Sgt. Pepper's
Lonely Hearts Club Band*, there emerged a group of established music
writers who began to champion rock as a "legitimate" musical form.
Pop records were no longer to be listened to and enjoyed but to be
dissected and analyzed. Gone were the days when you could earnestly
tell your friends that a particular song "has a good beat and you can
dance to it" (still one of the highest compliments you can pay); now you
had to talk about its antecedents in and its implications for the history
of Western culture. More than two decades later, we can state some
simple truths that we should have kept in mind all along: rock and roll
is not high art, song lyrics are not poetry, and the Beatles were not
descendants of Bach (they were, however, bigger than Jesus, but that's
another story). The "serious" music critics of the time had to find some
way to keep their cushy positions as self-conscious rock ascended. And
the Moody Blues were a perfect band to fuel the conceit.

With their second album, *Days of Future Passed*, the Moody Blues
broke new ground in pop. Never before had any band displayed such a
pompous approach to the seemingly straightforward act of putting
together a record. The first hint that this record wasn't going to have
your feet tapping the way their previous hit "Go Now" did was the
credit underneath the band's name on the cover: "With the London
Festival Orchestra, conducted by Peter Knight." Ladies and gentlemen, the birth of symphonic rock!

The LP consists of a suite of songs built around various parts of a day, a
diurnal concept similar to one that classical musicians had been doing
for centuries. The orchestra contributes much of the heavy-handedness
on *Days of Future Passed*, providing an overture for the work and
passages connecting the sections, labeled "Dawn," "The Morning,"
"Lunch Break," "The Afternoon," "Evening," and "Night." Unfortunately there is no break for a siesta. Keyboardist Michael Pinder
provides "Dawn Is a Feeling," which assures us that "this day will last a
thousand years." He must be talking about the day represented
throughout the album, because although this is the first song on the
record after the overture and assorted symphonic nonsense, the LP is
already beginning to feel like a day that will never end.

Hearkening back to school-day misreadings of Wordsworth and Coleridge, each of the other songs on the album displays a similar simpleminded romanticism. "Another Morning" is an evocation of carefree childhood. It strains to remind us that "Yesterday's dreams are tomorrow's sighs. Watch children playing, they seem so wise." Not exactly what we'd call an original concept or a good rhyme. "Tuesday Afternoon (Forever Afternoon?)" recalls the Romantic poets in its mysticism about Nature as the singer explains that "the trees are drawing me near. I've got to find out why." He goes on to describe himself as "swinging through the fairyland of love" and invites us to "come with me and see the beauty of Tuesday afternoon." Again, much of *Days of Future Passed* presents the Moody Blues' idealized world in terms more childish than childlike.

The big hit from the record was "Nights in White Satin," although it wasn't released as a single until more than four years after the LP release (in 1972, the Moodies were desperate for a Top Ten single). "Nights in White Satin" is a dreamy place that runs into the usual problems small brains face when they try to philosophize on the Meaning of Life in a pop song. Instead of presenting a clear vision that people can relate to on a personal level, the lyrics rely on trite phrases, like "Just what you want to be/You will be in the end," that sound more like U.S. Army recruitment slogans than a thought-out world view. Throughout the album, the orchestra relegates itself to conductor Knight's connecting pieces while the band sticks to the songs. But on the climactic "Nights in White Satin," the symphonic arrangement overwhelms the song: singer and conductor are in a contest to see who can be the most overwrought.

Days of Future Passed opens and closes with spoken doggerel passages that bookend the idea of night into day into night. On the jacket sleeve (words to both passages are printed), we can read this part of the introductory section: "Pinprick holes in a colourless sky/Let inspired figures of light pass by." On record, however, the stereotypical, classically trained bad-actor voice recites the second line as, "Let insipid figures of light pass by."

Not enough people let this insipid record pass by. Not only has it remained a "classic rock" favorite, but it was also one of the building blocks of the concept album, in which a performer in love with his own ideas erects a wobbly album around a slight idea that could usually be summed up in a single three-minute song. For that alone, the Moody Blues are guilty of a heinous crime against rock and roll.

JOHN TRAVOLTA
Travolta Fever
Midland International, 1978
highest chart position: number one hundred sixty-one

Before he was a movie star, John Travolta was a Sweat Hog. So it's not surprising that when his number came up as the latest actor without singing talent to make a record, he made one that sounded like it had been put together by folks who belonged in a remedial high-school class. His pre-*Grease* recordings are the usual bland pop outings we expect from a television personality with no particular interest in or affinity with rock and roll. But the future star of the film *Perfect* (another artifact—a movie about *Rolling Stone* magazine—with no connection to rock and roll) had something most other TV stars turned failed singers didn't have: fear of singing. The least important part of the arrangements on *Travolta Fever* is John's voice; it sounds like an afterthought.

Travolta Fever is a quickie double album meant to capitalize on John's success as the star of *Saturday Night Fever*. It is a repackage of the two albums Travolta made (1976's *John Travolta*, 1977's *Can't Let You Go*) before *Saturday Night Fever* catapulted him onto the cover of every tabloid in the land. Its anorectic pop with a beat bears little relation to the soft disco of the film.

These twenty-one songs (think of it: an hour of Travolta singing. Can't wait for the CD) split for the most part into David Cassidy wanna-bes like "Never Gonna Fall in Love Again" and Shaun Cassidy wanna-bes like "Razzamatazz" (sample genius rhyme: "Razzamatazz/All that jazz"). Since it's clear to the producers and arrangers (five are listed) that Travolta is just passing through and won't be around long enough to develop a style of his own (let alone learn how to sing), they satisfy everyone (except the listener) by aping other teenybopper stars. If they could have gotten Travolta to sound like the Archies, they would have done that too.

Travolta's sleepy number-ten hit "Let Her In" epitomized whatever little style he developed. His soft, sweet, breathy teen-idol voice wraps around a string-heavy orchestration and quickly loosens its grip. Travolta never bothers to get involved with the song: he has one eye on the lyric sheet (he probably never heard "Let Her In" before he entered the studio) and one eye on his watch. He did one take, tossed his headphones to the ground, and took off. At least we hope that all he

SIDE ONE

LET HER IN*
NEVER GONNA FALL IN LOVE AGAIN*
RAINBOWS*
A GIRL LIKE YOU*
RAZZAMATAZZ*

SIDE TWO

I DON'T KNOW WHAT I LIKE
  ABOUT YOU BABY*
BABY, I COULD BE SO GOOD
  AT LOVIN' YOU*
BIG TROUBLE*
IT HAD TO BE YOU*
GOOD NIGHT, MR. MOON*

SIDE THREE

SLOW DANCING†
YOU SET MY DREAMS TO MUSIC†
WHENEVER I'M AWAY FROM YOU**
SETTLE DOWN†
BACK DOORS CRYING†

SIDE FOUR

MOONLIGHT LADY*
ALL STRUNG OUT ON YOU†
CAN'T LET YOU GO*
EASY EVIL†
WHAT WOULD THEY SAY†
RIGHT TIME OF THE NIGHT††

*Produced by Bob Reno / Arranged by John Davis
*Produced by Jeff Barry / Arranged by Artie Butler
**Produced by Bob Reno and John Davis / Arranged by John Davis
†Produced by Jeff Barry / Arranged by Lor Crane

MTF-001

did was one take. Our fear is that it may have taken him days to open his mouth wide enough to be heard. At least Vinnie Barbarino would have sung loudly.

But the words put in his mouth by his hopeful Svengalis aren't worth being heard. When they want a big statement, they make him say, "You can't have rainbows without the rain" in the snoozy "Rainbows." In "Back Door Crying" Travolta talks of "polishing my wit." The only hint of what is to come is "All Strung Out on You," which sports a light arrangement that thinks it's disco.

Wait! Why are we wasting our time with the music on *Travolta Fever?* That's not what was important to the performer, the producer, or the audience. What matters is that this record comes with a large poster of the idol, suitable for framing. We wonder how many young girls bought the package, threw away the records, and pulled out their thumbtacks. A decade and change younger, and Travolta could have been a New Kid on the Block.

THE SHAGGS
Philosophy of the World
Third World, 1969
highest chart position: did not chart

THE SHAGGS
Shaggs' Own Thing
Red Rooster, 1982
highest chart position: ditto

Groups like the Shaggs are the perfect justification for a book like this: the group is fundamentally awful, yet you can't help loving them.

What's special about the songs of Dorothy Wiggin, as played by her and sisters Betty and Helen, is their straightforward pureness coupled with the trio's less than rudimentary instrumental ability. In their insistence that technical proficiency was immaterial, the Shaggs were the original punk rockers.

Unlike the punks' lack of chops, the minimalism of the Shaggs wasn't an act of will. "Going into the recording studio was all my father's idea," Dorothy told interviewer John DeAngelis fifteen years later. "We didn't feel like we were ready yet; we didn't feel that we knew that much about music." Indeed, the studio engineer suggested to Austin Wiggin, Jr., that his daughters might benefit from some practice before he shelled out the cash for studio time.

"Nope," answered the beaming father. "I want to get them while they're hot." All aspiring musicians should enjoy such a father's love.

Philosophy of the World, the band's debut, remains as epochal a record as its bold name suggests. Some bad records try to replicate a successful formula (either the artist's own or one stolen from someone else); some bad records try to stretch a performer's base. This bad record sounds like nothing else in the history of the universe. It's a true original: listen to it and you'll doubt that the Shaggs ever heard any music other than their own. You might also doubt that they were holding their instruments correctly. Recorded only months before Woodstock, *Philosophy of the World* revels in its insularity.

Oh yeah, we ought to tell you what it sounds like: two guitars and drums, all of them out of tune and playing different songs. Dorothy's lead lines struggle to keep close to her vocal, which wavers as far as a monotone will allow, and Helen's count-it-out drumming makes the Velvet Underground's Maureen Tucker sound like Gene Krupa. Her beat never wavers: no matter what song they're playing, Helen provides the same rhythm. The tunelessness of songs like "I'm So Happy When You're Near," "That Little Sports Car," and "Why Do I Feel?" has an undeniable amateur charm not unlike that of a grade-school band

191

plowing through "Pomp and Circumstance." Place this sound (noise?) atop a song like "My Pal Foot Foot" (the sad tale of a lost pet) and you're in talent-show hell. The Shaggs are incredibly sincere; for them, their minimalistic homilies are real life.

Most of *Shaggs' Own Thing* was recorded in 1975 in the same Massachusetts studio. History does not reveal whether they were confronted by the same dubious engineer. If he was there, he probably pulled Mr. Wiggin aside again and this time offered to pay for the girls' music lessons if they'd just leave. No such luck. The proud papa was even more willful: after all, the girls had quit school to concentrate on their musical development (don't worry, they got correspondence diplomas). In addition to more of their trademark, jaw-dropping originals, like "Gimme Dat Ding," "My Cutie," and an update of the Foot Foot saga, the Shaggs turned their talents to cover versions, most notably Tom T. Hall's nursery-school ditty "I Love." An atonal Dorothy recites Hall's list of lovable items (among them puppies, onions, and bourbon) with tremendous concentration, as if she's having trouble reading the lyrics and holding chords at the same time. It's a kitsch masterpiece.

A campy cult has grown around the Shaggs' charming, talent-free oeuvre, led by NRBQ's Terry Adams, an aficionado of the bizarre and the inexplicable who oversaw the reissue of both Shaggs records. In 1988 Adams put out *The Shaggs*, a sixty-eight-minute compact disc that contained both albums and a few extras. Stretched out so long, the Shaggs lead us to one conclusion: they are atrocious, but they are true originals. They will never be corrupted by the music industry.

"I'd like to continue with music lessons," Dorothy said in 1984, "but right now I'm pretty busy."

ANDERSON, BRUFORD, WAKEMAN, HOWE
Anderson, Bruford, Wakeman, Howe
Arista, 1989
highest chart position: number thirty

In the fifteen years after *Tales from Topographic Oceans* (relax, we'll get to it in a few pages), Yes members split up and reunited as quickly as someone could draw up a new contract. The most senseless of the permutations came in 1989.

It must have looked good on paper. Assemble four-fifths of the art-rock stalwarts who produced the group's only lasting seventies work (*Fragile, Close to the Edge*) and make a killing in the summer's reunion sweepstakes. Singer Jon Anderson, drummer Bill Bruford, keyboardist Rick Wakeman, and guitarist Steve Howe all shared an affinity for one another's work, but such respect often deteriorated into a performing situation in which no one communicated and no one challenged. On *Anderson, Bruford, Wakeman, Howe,* four musicians played their parts without coming into any contact, without establishing any common ground.

Anderson's lyrics were the same ol' cosmic sludge without the thrill of discovery which had once made them palatable. The music here is so complex, vague, and diffuse that it is easy to wonder if Anderson, Bruford, Wakeman, and Howe were playing different compositions at the same time. There was a reason this unit didn't have a name: it wasn't really a band. It was merely a group of individuals playing their own parts, each member blissfully unaware of any other's contributions.

Although no one we know listened to *Anderson, Bruford, Wakeman, Howe* more than once, the record did serve as the opening shot in an amusing war that rivaled the previous year's pathetic Roger Waters–Pink Floyd debacle. The question asked at the time was whether the Chris Squire-led band that held the legal right to the name Yes could possibly put out a worse record than this Yes (Not Yes).

Note: The obligatory money-grubbing reunion has since occurred.

QUEEN
Queen II
Elektra, 1974
highest chart position: number forty–nine

QUEEN
Queen Live Killers
Elektra, 1979
highest chart position: number sixteen

The British art-metal quartet Queen deteriorated into such an overblown spectacle that it's easy to forget that they were a truly malignant band from the start. They appeared in the early seventies as a sort of glam-rock take on Led Zeppelin; guitarist Brian May played heavy sub-Page riffs while drummer Roger Meddows-Taylor made tempo-wavering noise and bassist John Deacon tried to keep up. Meanwhile singer and occasional pianist Freddie Mercury cavorted across the stage in monochromatic leotards and looked like Mick Jagger impersonating Robert Plant.

Their most uproarious early record was *Queen II*. It may have been intended as a rock opera, but we're just guessing: song titles like "The Fairy Feller's Master Stroke" and "Ogre Battle" seemed to be part of some grand *Beowulf*-devolved good-versus-evil tale, but they don't make any sense, internal or related. What is being passed down to the new generation in "Father to Son"? What does the "White Queen" stand for? Why do the band members want to go to "The Seven Seas of Rhye"? Why do all four band members part their hair in the middle? None of these questions are answered. Perhaps the only reason we're sure *Queen II* is a concept album is that one side is labeled "Side White" and the other "Side Black." (Lucky for these geniuses they didn't have to worry about sideless CDs.)

Queen boasted on the sleeves of their early albums (among them *Queen II*) that "nobody played synthesizer." This really meant that nobody in the band had bothered to go out and buy one; the group's incessant overdubbing of more guitars, pianos, and harpsichords belied the "musical honesty" claim that usually accompanies units that are aggressively synth-free. A mass of any instrument can be just as misleading and false-sounding as a synthesizer, as Queen proves throughout *Queen II*. Whenever singers May or Mercury stumble near a note they can't reach, swirls of keyboards or guitars swoop in and take over. Of course if the group was less interested in showing off its vocal lines and more interested in a steady melody line that would promote the song, it wouldn't have this problem. But instead of being four members happily subordinating their individual egos for the collective benefits of a group, Queen has always been about taking turns in the spotlight. Live, each group member has a lengthy solo segment; each takes turns imploring, "Look at me!"

And it is when live that Queen's missteps have been most disastrous. They recorded some horrible studio records in the years after *Queen II*, including two with titles that trivialized the Marx Brothers (titles chosen, perhaps, in a fit of pique that the earlier foursome's parodies of highbrow music were intentional and effortless), but they didn't hit rock bottom until *Queen Live Killers*, recorded during a European tour in early 1979.

By 1979, much had changed for Queen. The future Sun City apologists had sold far more records (big hits included the hodgepodge "Bohemian Rhapsody" and the storm-trooper anthem "We Will Rock You"), they had gotten even lazier musically and started relying heavily on synthesizers, and Mercury had grown a mustache and formalized his Village People costume. Their music vacillated between airy classical rock and thickheaded hard rock, but by the time Mercury bellows, "Are you ready to rock? Are you ready to roll?" after only one song on *Queen Live Killers*, you know this is supposed to be a rock album.

No rock attitude, though. Mercury introduces "Death on Two Legs," the first song in a cabaretlike medley, as "This is about …," and the rest of his intro is loudly beeped out. Not that Mercury won't be gratuitously specific if he feels like it, as when he sings, "I suck your mind/You blow my head" in the unsubtle "Get Down Make Love." (Here's a brief swipe at fashion plate/stubble popularizer George Michael that we couldn't find another place for: the few parts of his career that Michael hasn't ripped off from Elton John he stole from Queen. His mild rockabilly "Faith" takes off from Queen's even milder "Crazy Little Thing Called Love"; his "I Want Your Sex" is a cross between "Get Down Make Love" and "Another One Bites the Dust." There: something else that's Queen's fault.) Elsewhere on *Queen Live Killers*, the quartet ruins its few passable rock riffs (like "Now I'm Here") with harmonic nonsense. It then collapses into an *a cappella* sing-along full of hoarse, off-key singing and Mercury joking, "Aah, the things you have to do for money."

To describe the climax of *Queen Live Killers*, we'd like to call upon the band's perky liner-note writer. "A single spotlight picks out Freddie at the piano singing the beginning of 'Bohemian Rhapsody,' which needs no introduction as Queen's biggest hit in Britain and Europe. It is unthinkable that the song could be omitted, although the classic multilayered 'operatic' section was a purely studio creation. Fiercely opposed to playing with any kind of backing tape, the group solves the problem in typically uncompromising Queen manner. They leave the stage and play the record."

Now that's integrity.

GENE CLARK, CHRIS HILLMAN, DAVID CROSBY, ROGER MC GUINN, MICHAEL CLARKE

Byrds

$15.98

BYRDS
Byrds
Asylum, 1973
highest chart position: number twenty

When you think of the Byrds, what comes to your mind? No, forget about the innumerable personnel changes that the band underwent during the late sixties and early seventies. We're talking about the sound of a jangling twelve-string Rickenbacker guitar and the high harmonies that made songs like "Mr. Tambourine Man," "Turn, Turn, Turn," "Eight Miles High," and "So You Want to Be a Rock 'n' Roll Star" the kind of hits that you want to hear again and again and again—and if you've read this far, you'll realize that not every hit is one that you want to hear again and again....

The original Byrds (Roger McGuinn, Gene Clark, David Crosby, Chris Hillman, and Michael Clarke) were more than just five individuals who came together to create a sort of hybrid rock and roll that crossed the rock side of Bob Dylan's folk with the folk leanings of the Beatles' rock; at their best they were a strong, insoluble whole. Unfortunately, by the time David Geffen offered them bakery trucks of dough to put their personal animosity behind them and record this 1973 reunion album, the spirit may have been willing—or at least greedy—but the talent was weak.

Instead of sounding anything like the group that put out a string of great albums back when McGuinn's first name was still Jim, *Byrds* comes across as a haphazard compilation of solo cuts by each of the individual members rather than as a group effort. The fact that they didn't even try to recapture the trademark sound of their heyday is a bit puzzling, but one can respect it: rather than getting themselves ready for the oldies route, perhaps they were looking ahead and trying to think up the ideas that would define a "new" Byrds. However, that reasoning fails to explain why the only thing they seem to be trying hard to do on this record is pretend that they're not even playing on the same cuts. Would you want to accompany David Crosby while he was singing a Joni Mitchell song? The band's fans got neither the old Byrds nor the new Byrds (whatever that was supposed to be) but a meltdown-ready piece of vinyl with the trusty brand name on it. The only thing the guys in the band got, on the other hand, was a chance to unload some of the stuff they wouldn't even put on their solo albums. That and the money.

McGuinn was in such a rush for that money that he traveled to the studio without packing his twelve-string Rickenbacker. By the time he got it shipped to him, the guys were already on the last minute of the last track, a cover version of Neil Young's "(See the Sky) About to Rain." After a false ending (stop teasing us already, guys), McGuinn plays a brief, overamplified line of thoughtlessness that makes us wish UPS weren't so dependable. In the place of McGuinn's Rick, the lead instrument of *Byrds* is Hillman's mandolin, which though functional is not nearly so distinctive. McGuinn's failings on *Byrds* aren't only in performing; he cowrote "Sweet Mary" with always-boring lyricist Jacques Levy.

David Crosby produced this, which is sort of like having all the great Yankees reunite and awarding the cleanup spot to Phil Rizzuto. Crosby is a born sideman; the few times he has gurgled up anything interesting has been as part of a larger group. Let him run the show and you'll soon find yourself peeking through a thin sound to find some half-assed political homilies much less sophisticated than what you'd find in *Pogo*. For example, Crosby uses this album's "Long Live the King" to introduce the Humpty Dumpty theory of monarchical succession. Since Crosby's production methods verge on megalomania, it's a topic he's probably long pondered.

Many listeners of *Byrds* did not get past the first track, "Full Circle," which limps out of the gate like a one-legged chestnut mare. The sound is listless, midtempo country rock, suggesting Pogo in a stupor. The words are middle-school clichés: "First you're up, then you're down.... First you're lost, then you're found." The only thing the Byrds lost on this record was their credibility; the only thing they found was the end of their record deal.

JETHRO TULL
Aqualung
Reprise, 1971 (reissued by Chrysalis)
highest chart position: number seven

Ambition is good. It encourages artists and would-be artists to reach farther, to explore and maybe even master new areas. Alas, ambitious performers who aren't starting from a firm base frequently come up with pretentious gibberish that alternately forces giggling and revulsion. If Emerson, Lake, and Palmer can't play rock and roll, for example, imagine what they can do to the classics!

Jethro Tull's leader Ian Anderson is one of those usually useless performers who can amuse us that much more when he tries to make a Big Statement, sort of like hearing Judd Nelson read poetry. Back in 1971, singer-songwriter-flautist Anderson came up with an idea he was convinced no one else in the history of Western civilization had ever pondered. Maybe, Anderson proposed, just maybe, there might be some problems with organized religion. Maybe, just maybe, he went on, there are more appropriate ways to serve a higher being than the ones Anderson learned when he was young.

No, Ian. You don't say. Like, wow.

Enough people were taken in by Anderson's awkward collage of fifteenth-hand theology, light-metal theatrics, and ill-informed rural nostalgia to make *Aqualung* an enormous hit among pretentious thirteen-year-olds of all ages. On *Aqualung*, Anderson and his band of merrie olde hacks plunder theologies, lyric ideas, and riff catalogues of anyone they can think of. This can be fun—some listenable bands have made careers out of aping other people—but not here, because Anderson's ideas and music are so cranky. Look at the back cover of *Aqualung* and you'll see a nine-verse pseudosacred text, penned in Gothic script by Anderson, starting with, "In the beginning Man created God; and in the image of Man created he him." Aside from the syntactic and theological nightmares implicit in those words, it's baffling why Anderson thought the text would be a good way to lure record buyers. Lyrics for the songs ("The graven image,/You know who/ With his plastic crucifix" from "My God") don't elucidate much more. Anderson is opinionated (fine), but also smug (not fine, especially when he's trying to convert listeners to his beliefs about beliefs). When you confront a song called "Hymn 43," what can you say but "Oh, my God"?

Aqualung chronicles Anderson's hatred of modern religion—although his vision is so limited, the only organized belief he attacks is Christianity—and the band leader's utter indifference to anything else. Anything else includes song form, arrangements, lyrics that make sense, flute playing that doesn't sound like an air-raid warning, and dramatic tension. Anderson plays up his ostensible English folk roots in the music, which does him no good. It forces comparisons with Fairport Convention, masterful folk-rock contemporaries who worked with similar ideas in fresh, exciting ways. (Anderson has periodically bribed members of Fairport Convention to join Jethro Tull and thereby lend him some tangential legitimacy.) In the same way, Anderson's romanticizing of preindustrial-era England—the time of the band's eponym, a famous agrarian—thuds false: his words impart no knowledge of what life was really like then, and besides, if he did live then, he never would have been able to fill arenas playing his ill-conceived homilies. Also, Anderson wouldn't have been able to have guitarist Martin Barre play heavy guitar riffs on "Aqualung," "Cross-Eyed Mary," and "Locomotive Breath" to assure radio play.

Anderson serves his songs well, performing them with the same over-the-top recklessness he brings to his songwriting. To approximate emotion when he sings, Anderson holds syllables too long and stretches words so long that they lose their meaning. Yet his singing is sublime compared to his flatulent reed playing. His grammar-school-band dexterity is the most heavy-metal aspect of Jethro Tull: Anderson acts as if he thinks that playing too fast and too loud will convince everyone that he is a genius.

For those of you wondering, a real aqualung is a kind of self-contained underwater breathing apparatus. Listen to this *Aqualung* and you'll get the bends. After all, Anderson's ideas here are all wet.

YES
Tales from Topographic Oceans
Atlantic, 1973
highest chart position: number six

"We were in Tokyo on tour and I had a few minutes to myself in the hotel room before the evening's concert. Leafing through Paramhansa Yoganda's *Autobiography of a Yogi*, I got caught up in the lengthy footnote on page 83. It described the four-part Shastric Scriptures which cover all aspects of religion and social life as well as fields like medicine and music, art and architecture. For some time, I had been searching for a theme for a large-scale composition...."

So begins singer Jon Anderson's ponderous liner notes to the most ponderous album by the most ponderous of all British art-rock groups, Yes. (Zzzzzzzz.) As you can judge from the above pseudo-explanatory excerpt, *Tales from Topographic Oceans* is a seventh-hand distillation of world thought, according to five of the most diffuse personalities (hence, when brought together, the most muddled thinkers) ever to try to coexist in a rock group. Keyboardist Rick Wakeman and drummer Alan White were the only genuine rockers of the bunch, although Wakeman's idea of inventiveness was often to try to coax fart noises out of his Hammond B-3 organ and White often seemed so bewildered by the band's elaborate nonarrangements that he neglected to keep a beat. Bassist Chris Squire was a frustrated guitar player who stuffed every open space in a song with too many notes, and guitarist Steve Howe's subclassical playing sought (successfully, alas) to distance itself irrevocably from the blues base of rock guitar. They topped this all off with Anderson's airy, high-register singing, which aimed to be innocent and childlike but in fact was insolent and childish. Anderson sprayed off Maslow-derived platitudes with all the comprehension and sincerity of a non–English speaker reading letters off a page. In other words, disaster was inevitable.

Tales from Topographic Oceans is a long, long, eighty-one-minute song broken into four sections (one per side on a double album). The wobbly sections have only tenuous connections, which break upon any serious inspection. The lyrics are Eastern mystical psychobabble (why don't British art rockers make fools of themselves with the blatherings of European philosophers? not as cool), heavily weighed down by dragging tempos. As soon as a song gets almost fast enough to garner interest, the drums immediately slip away and we're stuck with Anderson warbling ethereally about mountains or birds. The birds could fly away; the mountains weren't so lucky.

THE GRATEFUL DEAD
Europe '72
Warner Brothers, 1972
highest chart position: number twenty-four

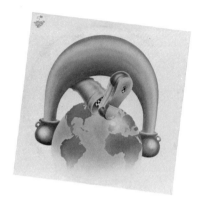

As much as we detest the Grateful Dead and their obnoxious, elitist cult, we have to concede that there have been a few isolated instances in which the standard-bearers of psychedelia haven't been a pox on rock and roll. Some of their early free-form explorations (particularly "Dark Star" on 1969's *Live/Dead*) actually went places, and they have lent their name to a variety of causes far more worthy than themselves. Most of all, we admire how they became rich and famous while circumventing the usual rock-star-making methods: the Grateful Dead are genuine grass-roots superstars.

That out of the way, we are happy to point out that more than ninety percent of what the Grateful Dead recorded is diffuse, bombastic, overly self-involved, and emotionally dishonest. Their popularity is inextricable from sixties nostalgia to the point where the accoutrements of a Grateful Dead performance (pot smoking, ill-fitting tie-dyed tee-shirts, hidden recording equipment, traffic jams) are more important than the soundtrack. We've had the misfortune of seeing the band twice, once early in high school when we were still smoking pot, once in college after we had stopped. Guess which time we thought they were better.

Europe '72 captures the Grateful Dead precisely at the moment they turned into a parody of themselves. By the time they arrived in London on April 2, 1972, they had taken their vision of extended jams as far as they could. What were they going to do, play longer? Also, personnel problems were seeing to it that they wouldn't discover a viable alternative to noodling until everyone, one by one, stopped playing. Ron "Pigpen" McKernan, a keyboard player and formidable singer and front man, was drinking himself to death: he embarked on the tour against doctor's orders and his body gave out within the year. Just as damaging was the addition of pianist Keith and singer Donna Godchaux into the fold, both of whom tranquilized the group's already softheaded arrangements. The back cover of *Europe '72* depicted a cartoon cretin pushing an ice-cream cone against his rainbow-colored hair. It was a perfect descriptive image for the set: messy, unnecessary, and, well, dopey-looking.

Did we mention that *Europe '72* was three records long? This is all excess, pointing out through repetition all the Grateful Dead's failings. Neither Jerry Garcia nor Bob Weir has the ability or the desire to sing lead for a rock-and-roll band, and the monochromatic performances defined by their weak, stiff voices are all sluggish tempos and aimless guitar solos that showed why the punks of half a decade later considered "mellow" and "tasty" to be epithets. These boogie jams (eight of the seventeen tracks meander for more than six minutes) leave the songs midway through the first verse and begin chasing their tails. Covers of songs from sources as disparate as Hank Williams and Elmore James sound drawn from the same spent well; you'd never know that Williams's "You Win Again" was country or that James's "It Hurts Me Too" was blues. It's just ... the Dead, man. Even worse than not being able to tell the songs apart, listeners can't even find the songs here. Its just solo, solo, puff, snort, solo, solo. Some have likened the Grateful Dead's jams to jazz, but for these folks jazz means they don't have to waste time with any structure. Just plug in and sack out.

The band wisely sticks to slow or middle tempos, because when they try to rock out, they strike out. On "One More Saturday Night," the group keeps playing faster and faster in an attempt to work up some steam, and Weir screams half an octave above his range, as if he thought that off-key yelling was a fair substitute for generating genuine excitement. The nadir here, though, is "Truckin'," all thirteen minutes of it. As in "One More Saturday Night," Weir yells "waaah" a lot, perhaps attempting to rouse himself from a nap. There are several noodling guitar solos, naturally, and the song eventually collapses into a jam, which turns into—another jam!—which turns into ... (you get the picture). The lines at the popcorn concessions during the succeeding jams, "Epilogue" and "Prelude" (the latter more than eight minutes), were probably monumental.

Because this version is so unremitting, it's "Truckin'" that takes the longest to dislodge from your brain after you've listened to *Europe '72*. The chorus of "Truckin'" offers the Grateful Dead's best-known couplet, "Sometimes the light's all shining on me/Other times I can barely see." This is the ultimate hippie profundity, which says much about the limitations of hippiedom: the best world view the band can offer is that sometimes it's on stage and sometimes it's not. And that insight takes thirteen minutes to play out! The Grateful Dead would spend the rest of the seventies and the eighties making records that ranged from indifferent to flat-out awful. Even Dead Heads admit that some of the band's live albums (*Dead Set, Steal Your Face*), were gratuitous. But rarely since *Europe '72* has a performance taken so long to end.

THE DOORS
Alive, She Cried

Elektra, 1983

highest chart position: number twenty-three

Jim Morrison is the most overrated performer in the history of rock and roll. Basing an entire career on the need to outrage easily affronted uptight folk, Morrison had no appreciable talent as anything other than a potential icon whose overwrought, overreaching lyrics and tormented, I'm-such-a-rebel posturings would have passed away with the sixties even if he himself hadn't.

As it turns out, dying was the canniest career move Morrison ever perpetrated: it has let him play Rimbaud to generations of kids who have never heard of Morrison's role model. (As the famous *Rolling Stone* cover proclaimed, "He's hot. He's sexy. He's dead." If not for the third fact, people might not consider the first two.) If we sound cynical, remember that practically every other aspect of his persona was invented. In early publicity materials for the Doors, Morrison established the myth that his parents were dead, concealing the fact that his last name was actually spelled Morrisson (changed, no doubt, for artistic reasons) and that not only were his parents very much alive, but his father was an admiral in the U.S. Navy. We understand that such an association in late-sixties America was an unwelcome one, but it's typical of Morrison's approach that instead of dealing with unpleasant issues he simply lied about them. We can only suppose that Morrison's image of himself as the Lizard King wouldn't have carried much weight if his fans knew there were a Lizard King Dad and Lizard Queen Mum back home.

In death, Morrison became everything he wanted to be in life, mainly because his own actions could no longer get in the way of his mythmaking. He became the anguished genius out of time, the unappreciated (forget for a moment the hit records and sold-out shows) poet who was persecuted and finally destroyed because of the intensity of his—you guessed it—art. Isn't romanticism wonderful? Especially when it fails to take into account a history of selfish behavior, drug and alcohol abuse, and general inability to find worth in others? Thanks to a new class of high-school boys each year who revel in self-deceptive images of rejection and isolation (not to mention needing a safe role model through which they can vicariously live out these fantasies), Morrison is remembered today more widely as a symbol than for what little he accomplished.

Alive, She Cried (you know it's the Doors because even the title is doggerel) is another in the seemingly endless parade of Doors product that Elektra continues to release to capitalize on Morrison's refusal to die as a commercial prospect. The album consists of nonstudio recordings made from 1968 to 1970 and focuses on the cheap theatrics and ho-hum sex fantasies that people are actually talking about when they describe Morrison as "dynamic."

The opening cut, a version of Van Morrison's Them classic "Gloria," is enough to make you want to run to the record store and tell the clerk you bought the record by mistake and please, please, could you exchange it. Recorded at a 1969 sound check, the Doors' "Gloria" starts off with little trouble, as the band sticks close to the original. Not surprisingly, things soon degenerate. Instead of continuing to play the song, the group instead plays what Jimbo thinks the song is about. That is—both literally and figuratively—one long blow job. The tempo slows down, then speeds up in an attempt to simulate the act, and Morrison yells, "It's getting harder!" between groans. This is Morrison at his truest: the only thing he cares about, musically or otherwise, is his own pleasure. Not surprisingly, we leave "Gloria" feeling unsatisfied and a little degraded. It's a bit hard to swallow.

According to the record's liner notes, the other cover version on *Alive, She Cried,* Willie Dixon's "Little Red Rooster," is an example of "the twisted country blues that became an increasing concern in their final days." We don't argue with the word "twisted," but this ain't Blind Willie McTell. The song in any incarnation is rather theatrical, but as usual Morrison goes well over the top when singing or, more precisely, acting out the roles. We would probably still understand the song if he didn't bark after the line "The dogs begin to bark and the hounds begin to howl." Only Morrison could take a song blatantly about sex and make it sound like a hunting day with the local noblemen. Morrison doesn't understand the blues because its gray areas don't jibe with his endless egomania.

"Little Red Rooster" is not the only cut that displays the sorry quality of the Doors' musicianship. Ray Manzarek's endless, droning organ solo in "Light My Fire" suggests that he's trying to perfect a new style of playing that involves elbows instead of fingers. John Densmore, as usual, suffers from DMPD, or drummer's multiple personality disorder. He can't decide which of the few simple rhythms he knows to use in a song, so he alternates among them until either the song is over or Morrison falls on his face and they might as well stop anyway.

Toward the end of Morrison's Doors days, many would show up at their concerts just to see what he would do next, the same way people go to stock-car races to see if Richard Petty will smash into a brick wall. Maybe they'd see Morrison carted away; maybe they'd get a freak show. They certainly weren't there to be part of that silly accoutrement, the music.

CHICAGO
Chicago® at Carnegie Hall
Columbia, 1972
highest chart position: number three

A four-record live set from Chicago: the very concept is enough to guarantee *Chicago® at Carnegie Hall* a position as one of rock and roll's all-time duds. The music on this three-hour blast of bombast lives down to expectations. The packaging, which apes a high-class opera package, is wishful thinking.

Chicago is now limping into its second quarter-century as a hugely popular purveyor of the blandest of sentimental pop ballads. (We're using the singular person for a reason: you may have half a dozen Chicago records in your collection, but we challenge you to name two of the members without looking at the credits. Chicago is a singularly faceless band.) Chicago comes up with the occasionally interesting single ("Wish You Were Here," a collaboration with the similarly erratic Beach Boys, is about the best), but repeated listening to its oeuvre reveals more than anything the band's fundamental rootlessness. Keyboardist and singer Robert Lamm envisioned Chicago as some kind of grand fusion of pop forms, but we can only guess at what those forms are. Chicago doesn't rock out, it has no funk, and it can't swing, which rules out rock and roll, soul, and jazz. There's not much left. (You wiseacres saying we left out country and western can sit down now, thank you very much.) All that you can discern in Chicago's formlessness are some big-band arrangements suggested by their three-piece, Bar Mitzvah-ready horn section and elements of the kind of Dixieland played by white people who couldn't find New Orleans on a map. With megaproducer James William Guercio—fresh from jazzing Blood, Sweat, and Tears into mega-tedium—calling most of the shots, it's possible that even some of the band members didn't know exactly what they were up to. Eventually they collapsed into a lowest common denominator pop group with overserious tenor Peter Cetera at the fore; he left the band in the mid-eighties, but the band kept cranking out elevator hits for fans too habituated to buying its records to stop.

Chicago® at Carnegie Hall was the band's fourth album and as long as the band's first three sets combined. (Their debut was a double album; from the start they didn't know when to shut up.) We can count all the great four-album sets in rock on zero fingers; except for a compilation that takes in a band's work over an extended period of time, such a length is fundamentally opposed to the brevity of most great rock.

Maybe the Rolling Stones or the Who, both at their respective live peaks around the time this was recorded, could have conjured up an extended live set worth preserving. But not Chicago.

You can tell that this set is going to be incessantly self-congratulatory from the moment already washed-up New York disc jockey Scott Muni begins his incoherent introduction (talk about trademarks) of the band by proclaiming "Success speaks for itself." This is the first of dozens of useless introductions on the record; the big problem is that most of them are musical. Lamm (whom guitarist Terry Kath labels "Mr. Chops") assays a meandering five-minute piano solo that suggests passages from a high-school performance of *Godspell* before the band slides into "Does Anybody Really Know What Time It Is?" Lengthy introductions mar the set so much (will they ever get on with the song already? you keep asking), you are certain the only reason they exist is to puff a double live album into one twice the length. Think of the songs as Vinyl Helper. How else to explain track listings like these:

It Better End Soon (1st Movement)
It Better End Soon (2nd Movement, Flute Solo)
It Better End Soon (3rd Movement, Guitar Solo)
It Better End Soon (4th Movement, Preach)
It Better End Soon (5th Movement)

You can imagine how long the damn thing lasts. And don't forget the seven-track suite "Ballet for a Girl in Buchannon" or a seven-minute song halfway through the set called "Introduction."

As with most bands who solo until the tape runs out (Emerson, Lake, and Palmer and their ilk), the members of Chicago go on separately because they can't communicate through their music. Attempts to bond with the audience fall flat ("We can feel you as well as see you and that's great") and the brief snippet of "I Am the Walrus" they toss into one song underlines how far this is from pop music. *Chicago® at Carnegie Hall* is a free-form jam by a group more interested in securing a trademark for its name (what did they want to do? sue Richard Daley?) than living up to its name, one of the richest musical cities in America. No wonder Cetera eventually left to sing duets with Amy Grant. It was a step up.

MILLI VANILLI
The Remix Album
Arista, 1990
highest chart position: number thirty-two

Some dreadful films make millions of dollars so producers can put together sequels that are even worse. (C'mon, there weren't any unanswered questions at the end of the original to justify *Young Guns II.*) These sequels regurgitate virtually the same plot as the original, make even more money, and encourage the producers to do the same thing over again (hence *Police Academy 6*). By the time summer rolls around, theaters are crammed with bad movies whose titles end in Roman numerals.

Lately the same lazy idea has been applied to pop music. It started during the disco years, when slightly different extended versions of dance-floor favorites could be sold to fans of the originals. Most were messes; those that have lasted, such as the grand mixes of insightful producer Arthur Baker, were rare exceptions.

The nadir of such recordings is the German duo Milli Vanilli's *The Remix Album* because it rechews the cud and spits out at us something that tasted horrible the first time. Their 1988 American debut album, *Girl You Know It's True*, was universally reviled for its flabby, twelfth-hand, soft Eurorhythms, its asinine sub-Hallmark lyrics, and the unctuous posturings and mechanical dance moves of its two corn-rowed singers, Robert Pilatus and Fab Morvan. It also sold nearly ten million albums and spawned four number-one singles.

Girl was horrible, but it filled a market gap. As strong a debut record as *Introducing the Hardline According to Terence Trent D'Arby* (1987) was, part of the reason it went platinum was that Terence had good hair and in his videos he knew how to work it. Making their move while D'Arby was obsessively studio hopping, Milli Vanilli emerged with not one but two D'Arby lookalikes who sported long semidreadlocks. Of course, because Milli Vanilli had to move quickly to capitalize on D'Arby's temporary absence from the scene, their coifs are hair extensions, not real dreads.

As lifeless as the singing was on *Girl*, the duo "sang" worse before an audience. Partially because they lip-synched live, rumor quickly spread that neither Pilatus nor Morvan (which one's Milli?) actually sang on the record, charges that spokesmilli Pilatus refuted with outbursts like this one in *Time:* "Musically, we are more talented than any Bob Dylan. Musically, we are more talented than Paul McCartney. Mick Jagger, his

215

lines are not clear. He don't know how he should produce a sound. I'm the new modern rock 'n' roll. I'm the new Elvis." Such brain-numbing, syntax-shattering eruptions led many to believe that not only did Milli Vanilli not sing on their own record, but it wasn't even them talking in interviews. This has come to be known as the Knucklehead Smiff Theory of Milli Vanilli.

Other competing theories prospered. Among the most popular were the Mirror Theory (they look so similar they must be the same person), the Disco-Eugenic Theory (somewhere in Munich someone clones mindless disco ducks), and the Obi-Wan-Kenobi-You're-Our-Only-Hope Hologram Theory (not only is it not them talking, they are not even physically there).

None of these hypotheses (we won't bother with the one that starts with their being named Milli Vanilli Mellencamp) accounted for the music, because no one paid any attention to that. Hence *The Remix Album.* Half the record is remixes, with the expected random echo, scratches, and synthesizer slashes that are supposed to indicate remixing. The other half ("Money," "Hush," "Can't You Feel My Love," and "Boy in the Tree") is made up of early tracks left off *Girl.* Imagine if you can the existence of songs not good enough to make it onto a Milli Vanilli record.

The producers' inside joke on *The Remix Album* is that the vocals (by whomever) are lost in all the mucking around and additional production. In that way, this set is a cynical hedge against those who claim Pilatus and Morvan are just mannequins: on this record the vocals don't matter. But when the words do bubble up, they are conveyed by singing so flat and groggy that even the poster boys might want people to think someone else's larynxes were the culprits.

PAT BOONE
Pat Boone
Dot, 1957
highest chart position: number twenty

Cover versions don't have to be bad. Some manage to capture the spirit of the original, and there are even the rare occasions when the cover is actually better than a notable original (such as Jimi Hendrix's version of "All Along the Watchtower," which was even better than Dylan's great version). What we despise is people trying to cash in on someone else's success by jumping in and stealing their thunder. (As we write this, two versions of "Black Velvet" are on the charts. We'll get to them in Volume 2.)

Although this practice now occurs with less frequency, it was standard during the fifties. Like too much else in this country, record charts were segregated into two categories: the pop charts were reserved primarily for the works of white performers, and the rhythm-and-blues or "race" charts tracked the records of black artists. While rock and roll was getting a stronghold in the R&B charts, it was making very little headway on pop charts because of who was recording it, not because of what it was. Pretty soon, record executives were having white singers do "socially acceptable" (industry lingo for "musically inferior") versions of successful records by blacks in order to grab a share of the bigger market. How else can you explain that Gale ("My Little Margie") Storm had a number-two hit with "I Hear You Knocking" in 1955 while Smiley Lewis's original didn't even make the pop charts— even though it reached number two on that other, secret chart?

The king of whitebread cover versions was Mr. White Bucks himself, Pat Boone. Boone's early career was almost schizophrenic in its attempt to pull together the various types of music that white kids were listening to during the mid-fifties. His self-titled debut album (well, maybe he didn't title it himself) contains covers of contemporary R&B hits bleached a paler shade of white. In addition there are the heavily orchestrated ballads that were making a desperate last stand against the incursion of that devil rock-and-roll music. Nowadays, when he's not whoring on home shopping channels, Pat claims that Little Richard would never have had a career were it not for him. Thanks for everything, Pat. You're a guy.

The ballads on *Pat Boone* are interesting only in that they provide the genetic link to daughter Debby's massive outpouring of ludicrous sentimentality twenty years later, "You Light Up My Life." The rock-

ULTRA HIGH FIDELITY
Dot
DLP-3012

Pat Boone

AIN'T THAT A SHAME · RICH IN LOVE · TWO HEARTS · NO OTHER ARMS · NOW I KNOW · GEE WHITTAKERS
AT MY FRONT DOOR · TAKE THE TIME · TUTTI FRUTTI · TRA-LA-LA · TENNESSEE SATURDAY NIGHT · I'LL BE HOME

and-roll songs point out the futility of a soulless performer trying to perform music that must come from a soul. Of the twelve cuts on the album, seven had previously been R&B hits, but just one listen to Pat singing, "Well, they call me a blues singer" on "Tra-La-La" is enough to tell you that no one with ears ever called him a blues singer.

Even after hearing them, it's still difficult to imagine Pat Boone singing "Ain't That a Shame" or "Tutti Frutti." He has no feeling for the songs: he tries to pitch each note perfectly (wrong!) and gives his voice a patently fake rough edge that he thinks matches the material. Although the arrangements smooth out the songs, what's most appalling about these covers is Boone's need to sanitize lyrics he thinks might be too "dirty" for his audience. On his version of the El Dorados' "At My Front Door" he sings, "If you got a little mama and you want to get along/Teach your little mama right from wrong," to fill in for the original's more provocative, "If you got a little mama and you want to keep her neat/Keep your little mama off my street."

The Boone method is to zero in on what gives an R&B hit its energy and make sure not to include that element in the cover version. Not only does he try to sanitize lyrics (we'll assume Little Richard didn't think the "rock to the east/rock to the west" lines in "Tutti Frutti" were about geography), but he also changes lyrics to make them more grammatically acceptable. As the liner notes reveal, "Wood [Randy Wood, who ran Dot] picks all of Pat's material [and] has had only one mild protest from Pat who wondered if it was O.K. to cut 'Ain't That a Shame' since it was ungrammatical. Pat still introduces the song as 'Isn't That a Shame.'"

Inconceivably (unless you have heard of the word *payola*), Boone's versions of "Ain't That a Shame" and "At My Front Door" were also sizable hits on the R&B charts. So even many of the people in the traditional R&B audience must have been more familiar with Boone's versions than the real ones. Had this situation been allowed to go on, we would be living in a very different world and one not nearly as much fun.

CROSBY, STILLS, NASH, AND YOUNG
American Dream
Atlantic, 1988
highest chart position: number sixteen

Give Neil Young some credit. When the cosmic songwriter-guitarist's old friends and testy ex-colleagues David Crosby, Stephen Stills, and Graham Nash showed up at his Northern California ranch to record with him for the first time in more than a decade, Young didn't laugh or turn away these desperate has-beens. He let them come in, probably fed them, let them touch his expensive recording equipment, gave them as much direction as they could fathom, and contributed a handful of songs nearly as vacuous and boring as those they'd arrived with. He repeated the pattern set when Young joined Crosby, Stills, and Nash briefly in 1969 to bring some muscle and edge to the anorectic velvet harmonies, but at least then CSN had the occasional idea among them that was worth recording. No more.

Young's contributions to *American Dream* were its biggest embarrassments, because Young was the only member of the quartet anyone had expected anything interesting from since 1974. We were (temporarily) so thankful that Crosby wasn't dead, we didn't mind that his contributions were slight and charmless, and we'd been afraid of Nash ever since he babbled on about mutant sponges in the *No Nukes* film. We didn't expect Crosby's postdrug lament, "Compass," to have any insight. We didn't expect Nash's "Clear Blue Skies" to come down from the ivory tower of smug liberal environmentalism. But Neil? His songs, especially the rambling, flute-sidetracked, semipolitical title tune and "Name of Love," were flops he'd never have dreamed of putting on his own records. Here, of course, they were highlights. Young has since noted that the only reason he agreed to take part in this record was that he promised Crosby a CSNY reunion if the selfish, appetite-driven freebaser cleaned up, but that doesn't excuse the quality of his own compositions.

If there's anything generous to write about *American Dream* (and we're stretching here), it's that the foursome's legendary overrated harmonies remained relatively intact. In a welcome surprise, Crosby's voice was particularly clear and unencumbered. (Of course by the time ol' Davy released his own album a few months later, the musically bankrupt *Oh Yes I Can*—not, by the way, a reference to Sammy Davis, Jr.'s first autobiography—that novelty had worn off.) But across fourteen deadened tracks that seemed to go on for weeks, it sounded like time wasted CSNY on the way. Young quickly moved on and revitalized his career with *Eldorado, Freedom,* and *Ragged Glory;* the other three resorted to playing at the Berlin Wall the week after it (like the trio long before) had became irrelevant. To a sparse, embarrassed audience that had had no warning that their protest was going to be co-opted, CSN huffed through an atrocious Nash tune they'd taken out of mothballs, a thing called "Chippin' Away" that had nothing to do with the Wall, but who cared when all that was important was pumping up what remained of a pitiful career? That, of course, was nothing new for Crosby, Stills, and Nash, who continue to jump at every opportunity, no matter how contrived, to trade in on their fleeting moment of early-seventies, brand-name glory.

BOB DYLAN
Self-Portrait
Columbia, 1970

highest chart position: number four

Let's play make-believe. Pretend you're
Bob Dylan. It's 1970. You had a dreadful motorcycle accident a few
years back. It left you close to dead. During your recovery period and
right after, you produced some of your strongest, most mature work,
like your collaboration with the Band, *The Basement Tapes*, and the
low-key masterpiece *John Wesley Harding*. The sixties are over, and
now that the Beatles are gone, everyone wants to know what the
reluctant spokesman of his generation is going to pull next. What would
you do?

Trust us: you wouldn't do what the real Bob did.

Fork over the bucks for Dylan's 1970 *Self-Portrait*, put the first side of
the double album ("A double album," you sigh, "just like *Blonde on
Blonde*") on your turntable, cue the kickoff track, "All the Tired
Horses," and hear … exactly what you don't deserve to confront on a
Dylan record: lush string arrangements, a lazy angelic choir, dumb
lyrics repeated until you want to drag those tired horses out of the sun
and into the glue factory. Oh yeah, and no Dylan.

WHAT!?! Dylan shows up, a bit sheepishly, on the second track (the
first of two versions of a country sleepwalk called "Alberta"), but it
sounds like the part of his brain that was shaken loose when his
motorcycle went out from under him finally fell out. The love song is
one-dimensional, but Bob's smoothed voice sounds distant from the
tale: even the performer can't conjure up interest in it. By the time the
song is over, his baritone bellow is so annoying that you're starting to
miss the choir. The most consistent accompaniment to *Self-Portrait* is
to the jaywalking country band on most of the tracks (the Band show
up for a few tunes, barely), not the female backup singers (angelic or
demonic? you make the call), but the sound of yourself asking, What
was he thinking? Dylan's previous album, *Nashville Skyline*, wasn't one
of his sturdiest, but it was an earnest attempt to accommodate his
songwriting and his voice to the relaxed rhythms of big-production
country, and some of its entries ("I Threw It All Away," "Lay Lady
Lay") have lasted.

If *Nashville Skyline* wasn't completely successful, at least all the tracks
on it sounded like they belonged together (or at least belonged
somewhere other than atop a magnetic bulk eraser). *Self-Portrait*, on

the other hand, was one of the most diffuse records a major rock artist had released since albums had become the main medium of expression a half-decade back. The only thing these performances had in common was that they weren't any good. *Self-Portrait* is (de)composed of haphazard originals, a few overrelaxed cuts accompanied by the Band, and songs by the mass of folk-rock songwriters who had all started as virtual Dylan clones.

When a "normal" person commits a heinous crime, forensic psychologists are called in to explain how it could have happened. This is precisely what rock criticism's equivalent of forensic psychologists, the staff of *Rolling Stone,* attempted in an unprecedented in-print symposium. Critic after critic fought for adjectives that could describe the misery within *Self-Portrait*'s grooves; the idea of betrayal was brought up more than once. A few suggested the record might be a joke, though no one could pinpoint exactly what the gag was. Even the experts couldn't figure it out.

For instance, those with the stamina to make it to side three had the misfortune of hearing Zimmy trying to replicate Paul Simon's celebration of puffy self-pity, "The Boxer." Dylan overdubs himself into a one-man Simon and Garfunkel (neither Dylan chooses to sing on key). But before you think this was just Dylan poking fun, remember that future *mbaqanga* rip-off artist Paul Simon was buddies with our hero. So if this was a takeoff, it crashed before getting off the ground, a private joke between Dylan and Simon too inside for us unfortunate listeners to comprehend.

This album represents the most precipitous drop, the most astonishing stumble by a major performer in rock-and-roll history (Elvis's fall was more gradual). Only four years after providing rock with its signature double album, *Blonde on Blonde,* Dylan now offered up what remains its most disappointing. Wasting expensive studio time to wax songs by Paul Simon and Gordon Lightfoot is as senseless as the surviving Beatles reuniting to record a tribute to the Knack. Dylan may have had some jumbled idea on *Self-Portrait* about defining himself in terms of his influence on others, but his song selection is random and horrid.

Then there's his singing. Bob's voice was never steady (his wildness on songs like "Subterranean Homesick Blues" and "From a Buick 6" is part of what we loved him for, after all), but here it's such an unstable collection of howls, it's easy to wonder if someone accidentally recorded him hollering for help after he got his hand caught in a car door. On some songs ("Alberta #1," "Let It Be Me"), Dylan sings the entire take as if he is about to sneeze. Dylan has gone on to make other abysmal studio records—*Street Legal, Saved, Down in the Groove,* and probably whatever his most recent one is by the time you read this—but he never again sank to the depths of *Self-Portrait.* The Beatles' breakup a few months before *Self-Portrait*'s release heralded the end of the sixties; *Self-Portrait* suggested the end of Bob Dylan.

In recent years, the Dylan cult has gone into contortions to claim that *Self-Portrait* is some kind of revealing personal and cultural statement, and recent live versions of some of its cuts, particularly the fine "I Forgot More Than You'll Ever Know" that Dylan performed with Tom Petty during their 1986 tour, lend almost an iota of credence to such notions. But let's look at the big picture (and we don't mean Dylan's ugly painting on the cover). Dylan has said repeatedly that he has never disavowed any of his records, but get this: when Knopf published *Writings and Drawings* in 1973, an ostensibly complete collection of Dylan's lyrics, the words from one album were mysteriously missing. Guess which record.

LOU REED
Metal Machine Music
RCA, 1975
highest chart position: did not chart

Ladies and gentlemen, we present: The Most Unlistenable Album in the History of Pop Music (including anything by Kenny Rogers)!

In 1975, Lou Reed had every reason to be in a good mood. It had been two years since the former singer and guitarist for the Velvet Underground scored his only hit single, "Walk on the Wild Side," but in the intervening time he had secured a loyal audience large enough to sustain him. In response, he tried to kill himself on record.

When most artists go into the recording studio, they do not intend to make a terrible record. Billy Joel, for example, is convinced that everything he records will make a lasting contribution to popular music, while others are content to put out unchallenging product their fans will simply enjoy. Lou Reed, ever the rebel, specifically set out to make a godawful record. By that criterion, *Metal Machine Music* is a total success. Reed didn't merely record something to infuriate people—that's something most rockers worth their Stratocasters should do from time to time—he ventured to release a slab of vinyl designed to make people scream.

Metal Machine Music is a 64:04 double album (each side clocks in at exactly 16:01) that lives up to Reed's liner-note claim: "No one I know has listened to it all the way through, including myself. It is not meant to be." Capturing a sequence of squawks, screeches, and squeals, Reed uses no instruments, just electronic effects. The same drone vacillates for as long as it takes you to take the disc off the turntable. The most complimentary thing that can be said about *Metal Machine Music* is that it doesn't get worse as it goes along (if you choose to be dragged along by it); it hits its stride at the very beginning and maintains the, er, tempo throughout all four sides. These pedestrian attempts at electronic art music make Phil Glass sound like Phil Spector.

As with most works of pop culture that fail completely, a cult has developed around *Metal Machine Music*. We imagine these cultists are the same people who have bothered to memorize every word of both *The Rocky Horror Picture Show* and its sequel, *Shock Treatment* (betcha didn't know there was a follow-up). Before we erase all memory of *Metal Machine Music*, let us add that some sort of special award should be given to *Metal Machine Music* mastering engineer Bob Ludwig, perhaps the only person without a long history of substance abuse who has listened to all four sides.

Metal Machine Music has been out of print virtually since it was released. When we called RCA and asked whether a CD reissue was in the works, we heard the phone drop and distant giggles before the line went dead. When we got a dial tone, we wondered for a moment if they were playing a newly remastered version over the phone for us. (At press time, an obscure British independent label had reissued *Metal Machine Music*, which goes to show you that there's a market for everything.)

ELVIS PRESLEY
Having Fun With Elvis on Stage
RCA, 1974

highest chart position: number one hundred thirty

Midway through the second side of *Having Fun with Elvis on Stage*, Elvis Presley cuts an ostensible joke short and asks himself, "What the heck was I gonna do?"

If we were Elvis (and we could be: together we weigh little more than the King did when he died), the first thing we'd do would be cut the microphones and make sure this record was never released. Unfortunately, Elvis's advisers at the time were his illegal-alien manager Colonel Tom Parker, his personal drugstore Dr. Nick, and the usual gang of sycophantic high-school pals, not us, so it did get out.

Presley was unquestionably rock and roll's greatest singer and its most important individual performer. Simply, there are no rock-and-roll performances that surpass Presley's in his heyday at Sun Records. Unfortunately, there are also fifty-odd soundtrack and live albums he "recorded" in the sixties and seventies that rank with the most hapless records ever issued. *Having Fun with Elvis on Stage* is the worst by a wide margin.

If we remember correctly, Elvis Presley was best known as a singer. He was not distinguished as a truck driver, electrician, soldier, actor, narcotics officer, or husband, all trades in which he dabbled. Nor was he known as a stand-up comic, and *Having Fun with Elvis on Stage* testifies why. This 1974 monstrosity was subtitled "A Talking Album Only," but it was packaged like a standard live album. There was only one minor problem: this live album had no songs on it, just the rote between-song patter, repetitious nonjokes, and flat-out stupid scarf disbursements that were epidemic at the King's arena shows in the seventies.

For most of the sixties, Colonel Parker, everyone's favorite Dutch uncle, made millions for himself (and, incidentally, for Elvis) by insisting that his client play interchangeable roles in interchangeable films. Eventually, people stopped paying money to see the same film with a slightly different title (*Blue Hawaii, Paradise Hawaiian Style*), although there was a certain campy pleasure at the end of the road, seeing Presley opposite Mary Tyler Moore—as a tormented, inner-city nun—in *A Change of Habit*. Besides, the former on-screen wife of Dick Van Dyke was one Petrie dish.

The conventional wisdom is that Presley pushed Parker to dump the movie strategy because he missed performing live. It's more complicated than that, but if the immediate result is as breathtaking as Presley's 1968 NBC-TV special, we won't split hairs. Presley then took his new live show to Las Vegas and, by the time *Having Fun with Elvis on Stage* was released, seventy-six of the country's largest sports arenas. Presley never played outside the U.S. because Colonel Parker, né Andreas van Kuijk, didn't want his foreign citizenship disclosed.

Parker, never missing a chance to make a buck on safe ground, saw to it that every Elvis concert was recorded. By 1974, Elvis's five years back onstage had yielded six live albums: *In Person at the International Hotel, On Stage—February 1970, That's the Way It Is, Elvis as Recorded at Madison Square Garden*, the double *Aloha from Hawaii via Satellite*, and *Recorded Live on Stage in Memphis*. Even if the set lists for the different shows varied, seven LPs of live material should have been more than enough to tell the whole story. (Bruce Springsteen, whose set list changed all the time, was able to document fairly comprehensively a decade's performances in only five records.) But no, that would have been sensible, and Parker was always around to prevent that.

The back cover of *Having Fun with Elvis on Stage* reads, "Executive Producer for this Recording Project: ELVIS," but this is a Tom Parker rip-off from the first, er, throat-clearing. Parker gives us forty minutes of slurred words (unfortunately, Dr. Nick's goodies were starting to kick in), sniffles, and condescension. Yet the condescension here is twofold. Not only does Elvis continually treat his audience like garbage, teasing desperate women who lust for sweaty scarves and pronouncing, "All of us onstage, we love playing music," but the record itself is a perfect vehicle for Parker to put Elvis in his place and at the same time make money for both of them (these shoulda-been-outtakes spent nearly two months on the *Billboard* album chart). Parker is as much the villain here as Presley.

Here are some of the key Quotations from Chairman Elvis that you will hear:

"Awwww yourself."

"I got wired the wrong way."

"Well …"

"You didn't know you were going to see a crazy man, did you?"

"Oh, wa!"

"I said, 'Huh?'"

"Well … Well, well, well, well, well. Well, well, well, well. Well, well."

"Look at these little red things in my pants here."

"On the piano, Mr. Colonel Parker."

"That made no sense at all. No sense at all."

"Ladies and gentlemen, I'm the NBC peacock."

"Well."

"I think my horse just left."

"England loves you?"

"Wa. Wa wa wa. Wa."

"I'd like to be relieved for a minute here."

"Well …"

"Well …"

(These quotations make even less sense in context.)

But wait! There's more! You'll also hear tasteless ethnic slurs! False accounts of his early years! Eleven different ways to pronounce *Memphis*! An Aunt Jemima imitation, complete with falsetto! Repeated demands to replay the ending of the previous song!

Finally, one of the many women on *Having Fun with Elvis on Stage* who demean themselves to gain a flimsy scarf offers up some spunk. "Gimme a scarf," she demands, and gets a laugh. We admire her audacity, but we wish she'd have followed it up by wrapping the scarf around Elvis's neck so he'd stop talking.

In the three sad years between the release of *Having Fun with Elvis on Stage* and his death, Presley made some truly horrible records that stand today as vivid arguments against barbiturates. But at least on those recordings, Elvis was ghastly in the context of performing a song. On this record, we don't even get to hear the music.

The Worst Rock and Rollers of All Time

You can't argue with the Beatles. They invented whole chunks of rock and roll, nearly all still remarkably fresh-sounding more than two decades after the band called it quits. There was a definite closure to their work when they parted; generations of bands have only begun to explore some of the possibilities of the Beatles' rich music.

One performer who hasn't even gotten that far is former Beatle Paul McCartney.

McCartney's solo career documents the increasing deterioration of a talent once thought to be indomitable. McCartney's twenty-odd records slide down a slickly produced mountain of dumb fun. He still hasn't hit bottom, but with each year he gets closer. If there's one thing that characterizes McCartney's wanderings in the solo wilderness, it's his refusal to address issues of musical or lyrical substance unless he has no choice. In his search for trivial fun, Paul McCartney has trivialized himself.

McCartney's first years on his own were erratic, but at least they showed the promise that he could conjure up something interesting without John Lennon around to act as a tough foil. *McCartney* (1970) was a low-key effort, recorded solo. Here McCartney's offhand, relaxed attitude was a virtue (not to mention an appropriate move after the studio perfectionism of *Abbey Road*). The usual annoyances were there—"Maybe I'm Amazed" was the expected latest entry in a series of inconsequential devotional ballads—but the record's at-home atmosphere dulled the pain. The same went for 1972's *Ram*, another relaxed outing characterized by less spare arrangements and an intermittently amusing and nagging hodgepodge in "Uncle Albert/Admiral Halsey." Hopeful fans considered these two records necessary head-clearing exercises; certainly McCartney would quickly work his way through this light stuff and return to material and ideas with more weight.

Hope was replaced by disappointment and then disgust when McCartney formed his new band Wings and put out *Wild Life* and *Red Rose Speedway. Wild Life* was even more tossed-off nonsense: what did you expect from a record whose meatiest track was called "Mumbo"? *Red Rose Speedway* sprang from the blandest moments of its predecessors. Its rockers sounded more like Sha Na Na parodies of Little Richard than the real thing that McCartney was capable of ("I'm Down"), and its centerpiece ballad "My Love" was a wet noodle in fans' faces. "My Love" set the pattern for what McCartney would now do for most of the time: it was a sloppy, first-idea-that-comes-to-mind love ballad without a hint of genuine emotion. McCartney's repeated moans in the chorus of "Whoa-whoa-whoa-whoa/Whoa-whoa-whoa-whoa/My love does it good" were about as convincing as his frequent claims that he felt more complete as a songwriter without ol' John holding him back. Who was he kidding? Apparently, most of us: both *Red Rose Speedway* and "My Love" went to number one.

Those few credulous fans remaining were sure that now he had finally jettisoned the nonthinking part of his brain, but by the end of 1973 it was clear that McCartney's legions would think up any lie to explain away his shortcomings and inconsistencies. As far back as his Quarrymen days, McCartney had an affinity for the blandest of English music-hall varieties (to be fair, so did John): he was always drawn to sentimentality, and the breakthrough success of "Yesterday" only encouraged his predilection. Even when McCartney was offering sharp singles like "Jet" and "Helen Wheels" off 1973's overrated *Band on the Run*, the good cuts lost their power when placed in context next to the usual slop. And of course most of the rockers (like "Rock Show" from 1975's *Venus and Mars*) lost their power once you paid close attention to their affected excitement. Besides, by the mid-seventies McCartney was much more at home with the whimsy of "Listen to What the Man Said," "Let 'Em In," and "With a Little Luck" than with all-out rock and roll. His 1976 tour, as captured ad nauseam on *Wings Over America*, was nice family entertainment, chock full of Beatles songs and laser displays. Only one true new rocker appeared on that three-record set ("Soily"); McCartney bored of it quickly and returned to hamming it up. Only as an established solo artist did he become the vacuous, always-smiling mop-top Brian Epstein wanted him to be.

In the years since that Wings tour, McCartney has veered between insubstantiality and unctuousness. His few attempts at seriousness (1982's *Tug of War*, 1989's *Flowers in the Dirt*) have failed. *Tug of War's* "Here Today," a farewell to the murdered Lennon, is just the sort of gratuitous melodrama that would have made John gag. *Flowers in the Dirt* is even more desperate, a collaboration with Elvis Costello that took no advantage of what could have been an ideal songwriting combination (Costello had the last laugh; he scored the far bigger hit—"Veronica"—from their partnership). The McCartney clique occasionally claims that Paul could be great if he was motivated; here he tried and simply could not cut it. We won't do more than mention McCartney's pair of self-congratulatory duets with Michael Jackson; they parody their softheaded images so completely we needn't bother.

When *Flowers in the Dirt* bombed, McCartney did what he usually does when he's in trouble: he coasted on the Beatles legend. Throughout the eighties he either recorded with his former comrades (Ringo and producer George Martin, neither doing anything of interest on their own, gladly signed up) or incessantly reminded us that, yes, he was once a really important person so we should pay attention to him. His 1984 vanity film *Give My Regards to Broad Street* (forgot about that one, didn't you?) was built around rerecordings of Beatles tunes, and when McCartney and his new band of unsympathetic journeymen hit the road to try to pump up some interest in *Flowers in the Dirt*, he put together a set (preserved for stupidity on the triple live album, *Tripping the Live Fantastic*, which features superfluous versions of songs like "I Saw Her Standing There" and "Birthday") that would barely exist without its plethora of Beatles tunes. Two long decades after the Beatles broke up, McCartney can't make a move without trading on the myth. And what he comes up with is an insult to its memory.

Please note that we never mentioned Linda or her one-finger synthesizer lines.

Runner-up
DURAN DURAN

MTV changed rock as surely and irrevoca-
bly as talkies changed the movie business. (Think of Christopher Cross
as the Marie Prevost of pop music.) The advent of music video meant
more than ever that bands not only had to play, but had to look great as
well. Music videos were welcomed so quickly and universally that a
new generation of performers took their cue from David Bowie and
spent as much time deliberating about how they looked as they did
about making music.

Some devoted much more time to their image. Some of these bands
were phenomenally successful in the short run but, because they had
no interest in rock, they disappeared just as swiftly. The fan clubs for
Haircut 100, A Flock of Seagulls, and Adam and the Ants no longer
have need for full-time employees. In keeping with tradition, the vast
majority of these image-over-music bands came from Great Britain.

No useless new fashion group (except perhaps the initial crop of VJs)
used MTV to its advantage more than the Birmingham quintet Duran
Duran. Fronted by a failed model who called himself Simon Le Bon
(Simon Le Bow Wow Wow was more like it), Duran Duran took the
image-packaging opportunities offered by the new medium and
exploited them to their unfortunate extreme. Their music, a simplifica-
tion of the intersection between New Romantic synthesizer music and
the most obvious elements of Chic-derived disco, wasn't important.
More than ten years after they first appalled us, we don't remember
what the songs sounded like, but we sure remember what they were
wearing in those glossy videos. The four songs that made them
designer superstars ("Planet Earth," "Girls on Film," "Hungry Like
the Wolf," and "Rio") are notable mostly for their scatterbrained visual
representations. "Girls on Film" is the one with the female mud
wrestlers; "Hungry Like the Wolf" is the one where Le Bon pretends
to be a Casanova Indiana Jones, etc.

The only thing that's distinctive about "Hungry Like the Wolf," their
first U.S. smash, is that it became a big hit only after it was remixed so
that the female screams on the chorus (pain or orgasm? depends on
whether she's listening to the song) were so loud that the song got lost
behind the sound effect. The only music you heard was Nick Rhodes's

you're-soaking-in-it, entry-level keyboard lines. It's no accident that the band took its name from a character in the B-minus movie *Barbarella*, an early Jane Fonda workout feature.

Although the band became icons in America as more and more homes were hooked up with cable, the members of Duran Duran confused their teenybopper success with the fruits of musical achievement. They were—you knew this was coming—artists. Some addlebrained music critics looking for hype to please their editors compared the Double-D's to the Beatles (both the Los Angeles *Times* and *Rolling Stone* ran "Fab Five" cover stories), so the group tried to live up to the headlines. One single pulled from the vaults, "Is There Something I Should Know," was patently *Beatlemania*-derivative, and lines like "You're about as easy as a nuclear war" indicated that their lyrical acumen had reached the level at which their ambition finally rivaled their incompetence. They even came up with obscure song titles, like "Union of the Snake," that meant less than zero upon investigation (that Bowie influence again). Anyway, most of them married models, no doubt for the conversation.

Then, like many performers before them, Duran Duran decided they wanted to be black. They had always admired Chic, and by now they could afford to hire Nile Rodgers and Bernard Edwards. (The pair's hits as performers had stopped, and both rationalized their new indentured servitude not only to the press but also to themselves.) Duran Duran's subsequent records ("The Reflex," "Wild Boys," etc.) had slightly less awkward rhythm tracks, and facile production tricks helped hide the group's innumerable shortcomings. The most prominent inadequacy—and the only one even those two master producers couldn't hide—was Le Bon's whiny vocals, which recalled nothing so much as the sounds of a man in constipatory pain.

Radio programmers too lazy to look for new hacks kept Duran Duran at the top of the charts, and the band's bank accounts bulged. So the band members had the freedom to embark upon—gulp!—long-delayed solo projects. Bassist John Taylor and guitarist Andy Taylor pulled fellow mannequin singer Robert Palmer out of obscurity and formed the T. Rex tribute band Power Station; the other three-fifths of the band formed Arcadia and put out *So Red the Rose*, a Duran Duran record without the pop hooks. Both endeavors earned out their advances within seconds of release (bolstered no doubt by confused videos that were intended to be surreal), and by the time the working vacation was over, the band was down to the three-piece core of bassist John Taylor (who had also written a song for the film $9^{1}/_{2}$ *Weeks*, another triumph of glossy sex marketing over substance), Le Bon, and Rhodes. The new lineup's first single, "Notorious," sported lines like "Don't monkey with the business," which suggested that they didn't spend any of their down time in writing workshops.

Follow-up singles stiffed, so Duran Duran tried to latch on to another dance-music fad, house music. Their last two hit singles, "I Don't Want Your Love" and "All She Wants Is," were desperate last gasps: they knew their time had passed (jeez, even ZZ Top were making better videos by then). The sound of Le Bon warning that he's about to "rock the house" produced only guffaws. One supposes Duranduran (as they were now billing themselves; it must have cost a fortune to print the new stationery) has recorded a lambada song just in case.

Duranduran's fall accelerated when a tour behind their album *Big Thing* turned out to be an extremely little thing. No longer playing arenas, they accepted bookings in mid-level theaters and ended up in clubs whose capacity was smaller than the guest lists the band enjoyed in the glory days. Of course, they claimed that they were getting back to their fans or roots or something like that, but few of Duranduran's legions were old enough to secure fake IDs. By the end of the tour, formerly dapper (albeit ridiculous) dresser Le Bon was reduced to wearing baseball caps and bandanas on his head, in a pathetic attempt to ape then-big-thing Axl Rose of Guns N' Roses. No tattoos, though.

Final proof that the group had nothing left to offer was the inevitable we-can't-think-of-anything-else-to-do-so-how-'bout-a-greatest-hits-record gesture. Thus the album *Decade*, which limped to a number sixty-seven slot on the pop chart before it crawled back into its originating hole. *Decayed* would have been a more appropriate title, although something that began life as a well-coiffed corpse can't decompose. Duran Duran (or Duranduran) made lots of money and satisfied the needs of girls waiting for Maurice Starr to put together New Kids on the Block, but their lack of lasting impact proves that no matter how cool your manager makes you look, eventually you have to think of something to say or you'll wind up in the cutout bin.

Runner-up
PHIL COLLINS

Former child star Phil Collins's first gig in
the entertainment business was as an extra in the concert sequence at
the end of the Beatles' *A Hard Day's Night*. With every minute since
then, his connection to rock and roll has become more tenuous. He
started in rock as a drummer for Genesis, one of the better art-rock
bands (i.e., they were boring only ninety percent of the time). When
the band's leader Peter Gabriel left for a far more interesting solo
career, Collins provided the bottom for many of his former bandmate's
tracks and along with Gabriel developed a breakthrough cymbal-free
drum sound. Alas, none of the energy Collins exhibited when Gabriel
was telling him what to do worked its way into any of the dozens of
other records Collins performed upon or produced, from Brand X to
Adam Ant.

Collins's tremendous commercial success has made him an inevitable
presence when major rock "events" show up at various stadiums in
England and America. He pulled his most gnawing shenanigan during
1985's transcontinental Live Aid megaconcert. After playing a short set
in London, Collins hopped a Concorde, flew across the Atlantic, and
within a matter of hours, performed the *same two songs* in Philadelphia. It isn't bad enough that he didn't bother to learn a third song
on the piano for the occasion or that he set a new entertainment
industry record by boring audiences on two continents in one day: his
silly, attention-getting gimmick turned what should have been a show
about helping people into a show about what stars do to help people.
Collins obviously has a big heart—from the Prince's Trust on down,
he's always contributed—but he was more connected to the events
than to the music he played at them.

As usual, Collins devoted time to the Knebworth '90 benefit concert
for promoting music therapy to help autistic children. A brief set with
Genesis (down to the trio—just like Duranduran—since 1978's inge-
niously titled ...*And Then There Were Three*) emphasized the most
obvious elements of their art-bubblegum mélange. They encored with
"Turn It On Again," a longtime concert standard. Dressed in Elwood
Blues shades and porkpie hat (we knew Collins shouldn't have hung
around backstage at the Atlantic Records anniversary concert), Collins
called for a breakdown, rapped a bit about how we ("we" meaning
fellow rich pop stars) all need love, and started singing "Everybody
Needs Somebody to Love."

Invoking the Blues Brothers was appropriate: that's probably the vehicle through which Collins first heard this Solomon Burke chestnut, and his connection to it is at best secondhand. "Everybody Needs Somebody to Love" led into a medley of instantly recognizable oldies: snatches of "(I Can't Get No) Satisfaction," "Twist and Shout," "Reach Out, I'll Be There," "You've Lost That Lovin' Feelin'" (during which Collins impersonated both Righteous Brothers: maybe he should have billed himself for this solemn event as the Self-Righteous Brother), "Pinball Wizard," and "In the Midnight Hour" parade in a hodgepodge before resolving back into "Turn It on Again." Each song accumulated more evidence of how foreign basic rock and roll had become to Collins. There was nothing in his mugging vocal performance to indicate that these crowd-pleasing standards meant anything to him. He was a professional entertainer, gladly offering what he thought the crowd wanted and eagerly accepting the applause earned by the song selection. The performance didn't matter.

Collins's eighties career as a superstar with an empty grin (inaugurated by his 1981 not-bad-but-wildly-overrated power ballad "In the Air Tonight") has been characterized by this desire to please. This desire is frequently at odds with the instincts behind lasting rock and roll. Collins's sentimental ballads for the films *Against All Odds* and *White Nights* are Whitney Houston music for people who think they like rock and roll. The drums are mixed high enough to make people think they can dance to it, and Collins's sentimental lyrics have inspired a generation of Hallmark employees.

Collins's ascendancy to superstardumb also reflects the mounting triviality of the topics he addresses in his music. This is not to suggest that he wasn't always frivolous. His 1981 hit with Genesis, "Abacab," got its title from the six chords in one sequence of the song (A, then B, etc.). The only problem is that Collins emotes the song with the same forced passion that suffuses all the other songs he sings. He doesn't care what a song is about. It can be about love, homelessness, a girl with a made-up name like Sussudio, or chord changes: he sings it all the same. That's why his album ...*But Seriously*, a blatant attempt to appear aware of a wide variety of social issues, is his most insubstantial effort. You just can't believe him. (The presence of David Crosby on backing vocals should have alerted informed consumers.)

He never stopped being an actor first, so it's no surprise that Collins's aren't-I-cute antics reach their peak on his videos, both with Genesis and on his own. In the "Invisible Touch" clip, Genesis members run after each other armed with video cameras. Unfortunately, nobody armed the band members with tripods (or instructions), so the result is just as unclear and self-indulgent as most of America's least funny home videos—not to mention the song. In the "Don't Lose My Number" video, our amiable hero deconstructs himself into self-parody. It's a video about making a video—the searching Collins prances through a variety of potential concepts, most of which parody either other videos or Akira Kurosawa films—but the result is Collins making a video doing many stupid things (picture the balding gnome as samurai). He thinks he's poking fun at music video clichés, but what he's really doing is forcing us to watch those same stupid ideas all over again. Like the Cheshire Cat, Phil Collins never stops smiling. And as with Carroll's disappearing cat, when you look closely at Phil, there's nothing there.

Winner
BILLY JOEL

Billy Joel started as Eric Carmen with a big mouthful of attitude. In the mid-seventies, Joel's songs "Piano Man" and "New York State of Mind" became enormous (and enormously influential) FM radio hits in spite of the tentativeness of their connection to rock and roll; Joel's piano-based MOR tunes seemed especially wimpish when compared to the heavy rock that normally fills stations with an AOR format. But they were minor songs from a minor artist, nothing more than reasons to change the dial.

As Joel became more popular (his 1977 *The Stranger* was the first of many platinum albums), his self-importance also grew. Even worse, he began to perceive himself as a rock and roller, a belief that bore no relation to his music, which remained predominantly smooth, Tin Pan Alley-derived pop. He had much more in common with Aaron Copland than with Aaron Neville. In interviews and onstage Joel started likening himself to fellow Tristater and genuine rocker Bruce Springsteen, a nervous comparison at best that only invited us to notice the obvious differences. For instance, onstage Springsteen would cover Elvis Presley songs, while Joel would do an impression of Springsteen. Which sounds more like rock and roll to you?

Around the same time, Joel began his love-hate affair with the rock press. He wanted critical respectability, although that eluded him until he became a pal to *Rolling Stone* tyrant Jann Wenner. Unable to understand how anyone could hear his music and not think it worthy of unadulterated praise, Joel began devoting more and more of his stage show to answering the critics. One journalist compared the introduction to a Joel song to "The Flight of the Bumble Bee," so for a time Joel would play the two back-to-back onstage and ask his audience what it thought. (Not that he would pay any heed if he didn't get the answer he expected.) Such babyishness also resulted in his shredding newspapers onstage if its reviewers dared to give him bad reviews. That showed 'em! (We initially didn't want to write about Joel because we were afraid he might strain himself ripping the binding of the book. Then we figured if he hurt his arm he might stay away from his piano for a while.) Joel's stage show (especially in the mid-seventies) was so pat and lifeless he would have had to add a full hour to his concerts if he wanted to rip apart all his negative notices.

Nobody paid Joel any attention when he said he was a rock and roller, so he figured he might be a bit more believable if he made at least a halfhearted attempt to record the damn stuff. (It was hard for him to claim that "Just the Way You Are" rocked.) Joel's first overt attempt to rock out was "Big Shot," from his 1978 LP *52nd Street*, an album whose cover pictures the hopeful rocker holding a trumpet in a decidedly non-rock pose. (Fifty-second street in Manhattan had been a legendary jazz cat's hangout.) "Big Shot" was Joel's attempt to claim for himself some of the surly energy of Elton John's inspired Rolling Stones rewrite "The Bitch Is Back," so Joel was at least two steps away from an original idea from the start. The lyrics were supposed to be sarcastic put-downs ("They were all impressed with your Halston dress/And the people that you knew at Elaine's/And the story of your latest success/Kept them so entertained"), but all they did was show how clumsy a writer Joel was in a straight rock context. So far so bad.

Something burned within Joel even after drowning in the bland sap of "Big Shot"; he still wanted to be a respected rocker and was going to waste an album proving it. We knew we were supposed to take *Glass Houses* (1980) seriously because on the cover he had a rock in his hand. The music was also made to appear as if it had toughened up; hack producer Phil Ramone pushed inattentive guitars up in the mix to approximate the sound of a rock record. Joel tried to sound tough on tracks like "You May Be Right" and "Sometimes a Fantasy," but he sounded petulant on the former and petulant and confused on the latter. It's as if Joel thought that the only way to rock was to act like a jerk: in "You May Be Right" his narrator presents a list of all the stupid things he's done lately and blames them on the woman who quite smartly wants nothing to do with him. Joel is so much an outsider that he thinks getting drunk and pumping your fist in the air is what rock is all about. He is especially mush-headed on "It's Still Rock and Roll to Me," a stuttering, knee-jerk attack on all the rock he doesn't understand (i.e., most of it).

Joel blabbed on about how *Glass Houses* was his rock legitimization move, but those who got past the album's package of bluster were confronted with the same MOR fodder: "Don't Ask Me Why" was only the most blatant of the soporific ready-mades that would put even James Taylor to sleep. Joel's first love obviously isn't rock. There's nothing wrong with that, but why does he have to keep lying to us?

Having failed at being the Rolling Stones, Joel tried to be the Beatles circa *Abbey Road* on his 1982 record *The Nylon Curtain.* All he did was get tangled. Tracks like "Pressure" and "Goodnight Saigon" were aural exercises, grand attempts to achieve sonically what he could never do emotionally in his music: create a believable, vivid world. *The Nylon Curtain,* its production derived from late-period Beatles and lyrically pretending to be Bruce Springsteen circa *Darkness on the Edge of Town,* was erratic. An honest take on the ravages of unemployment, "Allentown," is counteracted by the overblown, misconceived portrayal of the Vietnam War on "Goodnight Saigon." His big complaint: "We had no soft soap." (Wow, war *is* hell.) The next disaster was *An Innocent Man,* a facile dissection of various prepsychedelic, late fifties and early sixties pop styles (white doo-wop on "The Longest Time," specifically the Four Seasons on "Uptown Girl") that got the sound right but cut out all the soul and, well, innocence that gave the originals their enduring charm. Check out the video for "Uptown Girl" for evidence that dancing ability was not a mate-choosing criterion for either Joel or wife Christie Brinkley.

Then Joel committed his greatest musical sin: he decided he was bigger than rock and roll. His most recent studio records, 1986's *The Bridge* and 1989's *Storm Front,* are dense pop pastiches with one toe in rock and the rest in a variety of Broadway-derived pop styles. When he does make the requisite attempt to rock, as on the lame "Subterranean Homesick Blues" rip-off "We Didn't Start the Fire," he sounds forced, especially when rhyming "Adolf Eichmann" with *"Stranger in a Strange Land."* For "We Didn't Start the Fire," it's as if Joel listened to the radio one morning, decided that both rap and socially aware songs were hip, and decided to craft himself a polite entry in the field. (As with "You May Be Right" and many other of his songs, Joel phrases the song so as to deflect blame to others.) "I Go to Extremes" is a desperate attempt to sound more excited than the song really is; the title is the only thing about it that goes to extremes. Billy Joel claims to be a rock and roller, but his genuine rock cuts are rare and those few are too derivative to be taken seriously. And with someone of his popularity, that's far more than merely annoying.

The best way to understand Joel is to listen to his 1985 album, *Greatest Hits Volumes I and II*. Over the course of thirteen years and his first twelve albums, Joel had produced enough respectable material to fill a brief, solid retrospective. This was not it. At his "greatest," Joel is a talented craftsman, fashioning marginally agreeable pop from expected sources. *Greatest Hits Volumes I and II* was a marketing tool that augmented Joel's commerical smashes with a pair of new tracks to lure those who had already purchased the hits. One of the new songs on the compilation was "You're Only Human (Second Wind)," a nightmarish mush of be-all-you-can-be pop psychology, complete with one of the least spontaneous-sounding vocal mistakes ever perpetrated on vinyl. To respond to Joel's inevitable complaint that the mistake was indeed spontaneous, the idea in rock and roll is to *sound* spontaneous, not merely *be* spontaneous. Billy's protests don't matter because the moment sounds fake. No single performer has done more to encourage musicians without a shred of rock credibility to think that pretending to rock out is the same thing as rocking out than Billy Joel.

Jimmy Guterman is the author of several books, among them *12 Days on the Road*; he has written for *Rolling Stone, Spy,* and a variety of other publications. **Owen O'Donnell** has worked in publishing since graduating from college in 1982. He is the editor of *Contemporary Theater, Film, and Television.*

Jimmy and Owen grew up around the block from each other in Bayonne, New Jersey. Both have a sick love and a keen eye for rock-and-roll trash. This book is the climax of more than a decade of scouring used record stores for the world's most unintentionally hilarious records. Also it's a chance to earn back some of the money they've wasted on Queen records.

They are threatening to write another book together.